The Essential Buyer's Guide

VOLKSWAGEN
BUS

Your marque experts: Ken Cservenka & Richard Copping

VELOCE PUBLISHING
THE PUBLISHER OF FINE AUTOMOTIVE BOOKS

www.veloce.co.uk

For post publication news, updates and amendments relating to this book please visit www.veloce.co.uk/books/V4022

First published in December 2005, reprinted May 2007, June 2008, Febuary 2010, March 2012 and May 2015 by Veloce Publishing Limited, Veloce House, Parkway Farm Business Park, Middle Farm Way, Poundbury, Dorchester, Dorset, DT1 3AR, England.
Fax 01305 250479/e-mail info@veloce.co.uk/web www.veloce.co.uk or www.velocebooks.com.
ISBN: 978-1-845840-22-8 UPC: 6-36847-04022-2

Readers with ideas for automotive books, or books on other transport or related hobby subjects, are invited to write to the editorial director of Veloce Publishing at the above address.
British Library Cataloguing in Publication Data – A catalogue record for this book is available from the British Library.
Typesetting, design and page make-up all by Veloce Publishing Ltd on Apple Mac. Printed in India by Replika Press.

Congratulations! By purchasing this book, you are halfway to becoming the owner of today's most popular classic Volkswagen.

We are looking at 40 years of production, and three distinct generations of Bus. We are also endeavouring to cover the wide range of models available, from workaday Panelvans and Pickups, to the more upmarket people carriers. Additionally, we refer to camper conversions, from official to homespun options. The only way we can cover such a vast range is because, whatever its suit of clothes, a Bus is still a Bus, and between the product of 1950 and 1979 (and to a lesser extent that of 1990) each is a Volkswagen and built in a similar style.

While Volkswagen in Europe tended to refer to the Bus by its various model names, such as the Micro Bus De Luxe for the top-of-the-range passenger-carrying option, the USA devised its own names, most notably the Campmobile for the Campervan and the Vanagon for the third-generation models. The enthusiast scene has bestowed terms of endearment on the first two Buses, the original one (1950-1967) being widely known as the Splittie, thanks to its two-pane windscreen and the second as the Bay (1968-1979), owing to its seemingly panoramic front screen. Subsequent generations are simply referred to by their type number.

Splitties and Bays have few if any detractors, but the same cannot be said with confidence of the T3 (also known as the T25 on occasion in the UK). Possibly the least coveted of any generation, we'll nevertheless guide you towards finding an example that you can be proud of and one that is genuinely worth the money you are likely to pay for it. With pre-1979 Bus prices still ever-increasing after what is now a lengthy period, we would say that if you buy at a price under our guidelines you've done really well (as long as it really meets our criteria of soundness). If you're over, all it might prove is that somebody's investment is already paying the handsome dividend you too can expect over the next few years.

Ken Cservenka & Richard Copping

This Splittie dates from February 1963 and, although a camper now, started life as a Kombi.

Dating from the autumn of 1972, this Bay has a twin-port 1600 engine, and is finished in Pastel White over Niagara Blue.

This classic 2-litre T3 can be identified as an air-cooled model by the single 'grille' on the front.

Contents

Essential Buyer's Guide™ currency

At the time of publication a BG unit of currency "●" equals approximately £1.00/ US$1.48/Euro 1.39. Please adjust to suit current exchange rates.

Is it the vehicle for you?
– marriage guidance

Tall and short drivers
As long as you remember that the Bus is essentially a glorified commercial vehicle, even in Deluxe mode, and you're not 'vertically challenged', you'll be OK.

Weight of controls
We have heard people complain that a Bus is heavy and difficult to drive; but after all, this was never intended to be a small family runabout!

Will it fit in the garage?
Rather unlikely, unless you've had the garage purpose-built. Length might be OK. Height, at around 1925mm for the Splittie and 1950mm plus for the T3, could be a problem.

Interior space
How was it described originally? Ah yes, a 'box on wheels'. Loads of room, although a holiday in a Pickup could be interesting!

Luggage capacity
Will 750kg for the earliest basic Panelvan do?

Running costs
Let's be honest, you're not going to get far on a tank of fuel. Fortunately for the 'resto buffs', though, parts are comparatively cheap for most ages of Bus, with some panels being re-manufactured to meet demand.

Usability
Pedestrian performance is a certainty with a Splittie that doesn't have a 1500cc engine. Even 1600 Bays have been criticised, while 1600 heavyweight T3 models struggle. Realistically, few would opt to use any of the first three generations of Bus as a daily driver However, all but the pre-1961 model Splitties are ideal for relaxing holidays and weekends out and about.

Parts availability
Most items are readily available, thanks in part to shared Beetle ancestry. Also, due to popularity, a good market has grown in reproduction parts, some of which are (almost) as good as new old-stock items.

Parts cost
Reasonable, with plenty of aftermarket options. Certain early items will inevitably command premium prices.

Insurance group
Enthusiasts would recommend an agreed value classic policy with a realistic mileage limitation. Insurance shouldn't cost a fortune.

Investment potential
Anyone buying a Splittie 10 years ago and selling it today could expect a very handsome profit indeed. Bays are becoming pricey, too; you might find a bargain still, but there are some dogs about that could cost a lot to bring up to scratch. The T3's press remains mixed and market prices reflect this. There did seem a time when the trend was upward, but the ever-increasing popularity of subsequent generations appears to have resulted in little or no movement for some years.

Foibles
Painfully slow before the mid-1960s. Later, VW's insistence on retaining the 1600 engine caused a great deal of heartache for those having to push their Buses up the slightest incline. The 'aerodynamics of a brick' applies even to the T3.

Plus points
A cult vehicle, loved from the start by successive generations and with every sign that newer models won't lose out longer-term either. Air-cooled longevity, distinctive, a fun classic, with 'cool' camping options!

Minus points
Escalating prices for earlier models, with second mortgage figures being demanded. What use is a Panelvan or Pickup? Worse still, a mobile shop or an ambulance! Six-volt electrics on pre-1967 model year vehicles. Tin worm, when compared to a Beetle, for example, potentially more extensive and certainly more life threatening.

Alternatives
There's simply nothing in the same league as the early Buses. There are bigger, less pricey options around, but we're not naming them, because we wouldn't buy them!

A high driving position gives a commanding view of the road.

Cost considerations
– affordable, or a money pit?

VW recommends the following service intervals:
Every 3000 and 6000 miles, or once a year minimum for most lubrication and adjustment cycles, with 30,000 miles, or every three years, added for transmission and brake fluid changes. Later water-cooled and diesel T3 models have longer service intervals and lubricated-for-life gearboxes.

Small service: ⬤ x70 from independent VW specialists
Large service: ⬤ x160 from independent VW specialists
New clutch: (not fitted) ⬤ x85-⬤ x120; (fitted) ⬤ x200
Rebuilt engine: (not fitted) air-cooled 1600 ⬤ x1300; air-cooled, 2-litre, water-boxer, and diesel from ⬤ x2300
Cylinder heads: (each not fitted) 1600 air-cooled ⬤ x200; 2-litre air-cooled ⬤ x290; T3 1.9-2.1 water-boxer ⬤ x335
Rebuilt gearbox: 1950 ⬤ x1400; 1960 ⬤ x700; 1970 ⬤ x750; Auto ⬤ from x1000 if you can find one
Brake drum: Bay front ⬤ x80; Bay rear ⬤ x80; T3 rear from ⬤ x60
Brake disc: Bay ⬤ from x44
Brake pad: Bay 71-79 from ⬤ x18; T3 79-91 from ⬤ x18-x26
Brake shoes: Splittie front 52-62 ⬤ x50; rear 52-62 ⬤ x38
Brake shoes: Splittie front 63-67 ⬤ x30; rear 63-67 ⬤ x30
Brake shoes: Bay front 68-72 ⬤ x32; rear 68-72 ⬤ x30; 72-79 ⬤ x30
Brake shoes: T3 rear ⬤ x35
New headlight: Bay 68-73 ⬤ x98; 74-79 Hella ⬤ x40
Front axle beam: from ⬤ x450
Brake calliper: Bay pair German from ⬤ x150
Exhaust system (not fitted): Bay from ⬤ x130
Exhaust system (not fitted): T3 air-cooled 1600 from ⬤ x450
Exhaust system (not fitted): T3 air-cooled 2000 from ⬤ x145
Exhaust system (not fitted): T3 water-boxer from ⬤ x450
Exhaust system (not fitted): T3 Diesel from ⬤ x125
Steering box: Bay 73-79 ⬤ x175
Steering rack: T3 ⬤ x95; Power steering rack ⬤ x425
Bumpers: Bay 73-79 ⬤ x94; T3 from ⬤ x80 with end caps
LHD to RHD conversion (don't do it): from ⬤ x1000
Twin Weber or Dellorto kit to replace original Solex: ⬤ x800
Complete body restoration: from ⬤ x4000
Full re-spray (including preparation): from ⬤ x3500
Full professional restoration from basket case: from ⬤ x7500

Parts that are easy to find: Body parts for later Buses, service items, most late model trim and seals, engine parts Bays and T3.

Parts that are hard to find: Transmission parts for Automatic (an option from 1973 onwards), NOS early body and chassis parts, NOS early light units, Splittie and Bay steering box, 30bhp or early 34bhp engines.

Parts that are very expensive: Splittie and early Bay bumpers, Splittie and Bay steering box, Westfalia camper pop-up roof canvas, early rear lights, semaphores, early trim and switches, T3 Water-boxer and Diesel cylinder heads.

A new clutch will set you back between ● x85 and ● x120 dependent on model and if you fit it yourself.

A new headlight reflector for a Splittie will cost around ● x118 and a complete 'fish eye' indicator ● x35.

Living with a Bus
– will you get along together?

First, let's get the workhorse models out of the way. Unless you're buying a Pickup or a Panelvan to do a serious job of work for your business, which in the case of the Splittie or Bay seems highly unlikely for reasons of age, they are not something most would opt to live with as either a daily or regular use vehicle. In T3 form we could imagine a jobbing builder paying a small sum to buy a mid-1980s Pickup runner with a six month life expectancy, but we doubt very much if he will be reading this guide. No, if you're contemplating an Ambulance, a Disaster Support Vehicle, or plain Panelvan, you are seriously into the show, or specialist scene and we'd expect you to be living with another vehicle on a daily basis.

Plenty of room in this Splittie delivery van, but for what practical purpose to today's owner?

Few would seriously consider any Splittie a practical mode of daily transport, while Buses produced in the 1950s tend to fall strictly into the 'for show purposes only' category. A 1960s Microbus Deluxe (known by enthusiasts as a Samba) the forerunner of the people carriers of today, might offer a limited degree of practicality, but its age and high value suggest that it would be much better kept locked away in its own purpose-built garage, only to surface on balmy summer days. The same applies to the slightly more basic Microbus and the dual-purpose delivery van/ people carrier, the Kombi. All Splitties, other than those manufactured in the final year of production (1967 model year), featured less than practical six-volt electrics and, until the mid-1960s, were powered by a 34bhp, 1200 engine.

The Bay was launched in the summer of 1967 (1968 model year) and represented a major leap forward; so much so, in fact, that it might still be compatible with many aspects of modern motoring. If a leisurely pace is acceptable (a hallmark of all 1600 engine models) drivers of Bays could use their vehicles on a daily basis, particularly if there is no great wish to show the product in a Concours line-up. Although values are definitely on the up, some might still consider all-year round usage of a Bay acceptable. However, the acres of bare painted metal at the

vehicle's front (think stone-chips) and the lack of built in anti-rust treatment, inevitably mean a constant battle to keep the bodywork up to scratch if the Bus is driven throughout the winter months in the UK. When you consider the cost of a brand new Bus, though, and the inevitable spiral of depreciation, the thought of spending money each year to keep a Bay up to scratch sounds

All camper conversions are ideal for leisurely weekends away.

reasonably attractive, considering the product's classic status and appeal.

Although the T3 was endowed with additional protection against rust in 1985, its vulnerability to the ravages of the tin-worm as far as panel seams go is well-known. Sadly, its stylistic appeal is limited by the fact that it doesn't exhibit the retro-charm of its predecessors, although a carefully modified or enhanced Camper should attract a small crowd of admirers. It's more practical than a Splittie, but falls short of its successors in too many ways.

No depreciation with a Bay, increasing in value and rust-free examples easily obtained.

The most practical of all Bus options has to be the Camper (even if it's a Splittie). Once manufacturers got into the swing of converting the Kombi, Microbus and, occasionally, the Microbus Deluxe (realistically we mean 1960s onwards) the Bus became the ideal vehicle to live with, and far superior to any offering produced by another manufacturer. Relatively high fuel consumption and leisurely performance don't matter in the slightest, because the Bus' role is to be a weekend retreat, a relaxed holiday home, and cheap B&B for the show addict. Campers attract campers and there's a great club community out there just waiting to welcome you on board

A forerunner of the popular people carriers of today and eminently luxurious.

as part of the team. One word of warning, though, there's a myriad of conversions. Don't rush and buy the first camper you see; however sound the bodywork and low the mileage. Some sleep two and are basic in what they offer, while others are fun for all the family, with every conceivable luxury thrown in for good measure! Read and digest what we have to say, and compare a few models at the next VW show.

Finally, for those whose idea of living with a Bus isn't either to drive it, or enjoy the camping scene, but rather to tinker with it in the garage, well you're in luck, at least as far as the Splittie and Bay go, with their air-cooled simplicity and relative ease of restoration.

Relative values
– which model for you?

See the 'What's it worth to you' chapter for value assessment. This chapter shows, in percentage terms, the value of individual models in good condition. Concours Buses (as good or better than new) will be worth nearly double, while restoration projects will be worth around a tenth.

Range availability

March 1950	Panelvan (or delivery van).
June 1950	Kombi (a basic people carrier, with easily removable seats). Doubles as a delivery van, with three additional windows per side.
June 1950	Microbus (the first true people carrier with permanent seating).
June 1951	Microbus Deluxe (known by enthusiasts as the Samba). Distinguishable by skylight windows, additional bright-work, and a full-length, folding canvas sunroof).
August 1952	Pickup.
November 1958	Double or Crew-cab Pickup (a multi-tasking six or three-seater with additional carrying capacity cab, coupled to a shortened flat bed).
September 1961	High Roof, or High Top Delivery Van.

When Splittie production ceased in July 1967, all options were immediately available with the new Bay body shape. The Microbus Deluxe was briefly referred to as the Clipper before becoming the Microbus L. In August 1972, a three-speed automatic (extra cost) option became available for all but the Pickup. Fuel injection became standard in the US with the introduction of an 1800cc engine for the 1974 model year.

Bay production ceased in July 1979. Initially, the new T3 range was as before, although, over the years, a wider variety of seat options had emerged (seven, eight and nine). In 1981, a new super Deluxe model, the seven-seater Caravelle was launched. Rebranding led to lowlier versions being known as Transporters and people carriers as Caravelles (US marketing had already seen the T3 termed the Vanagon). There was also a special luxury Caravelle, known as the 'Carat'. February 1985 saw the launch of a permanent all-wheel drive 'Syncro'. 1986 saw the arrival of the Multivan, a combination of Bus and Camper, built initially by the coachbuilders Westfalia and later by VW itself. This move finally confirmed the Camper as an integral part of the range. T3s were replaced by the T4 in 1990, but some variants continued in production until 1992.

Campers

Many buyers will opt for a Camper. For many years, campers were not part of the official range. Instead, manufacturers based their own packages on one of the VW models, invariably the Kombi or Microbus, and occasionally, the Microbus Deluxe. The German firm of Westfalia, with its Camping Box launched at the start of the 1950s, was the innovator. Links with VW, particularly in the USA, remained strong. In the UK, the Devon range was launched in 1957. Other well-known names include Autohome, Canterbury Pitt, Danbury, and Dormobile. In the USA, Andrews Inc of Indiana got in on the act with the Sportsmobile, while in Germany, Karmann produced a VW camper with a caravan body.

A camper conversion – always the most expensive option.

1950 to March 1955 – 'Barn door' Splitties

From launch until March 1955, the Splittie had an enormous engine lid, hence the 'barn door' nickname. Initially capable of just 50mph, thanks to the 25bhp engine borrowed from the Beetle, they featured a crash gearbox until March 1953. Incredibly rare, and worth a great deal of money, nearly all were LHD. These Buses are really the preserve of the dedicated enthusiast and restorer.
150%

The 'barn door' Splittie, pre-March 1955.

March 1955 to July 1967 – Splittie

The face-lifted Splittie featured a 'peak cap' overhang at the front, and had better cab ventilation, a full-length dash on all models, and a much smaller engine lid. A 30bhp engine was used from March 1955. This received a much needed revamp in 1959 featuring a stronger crankshaft, redesigned valve gear and a crankcase that resembled the 34bhp unit, which followed from June 1960, whereupon a 34bhp engine was fitted. European models had semaphores until mid-1960 (US until 1955), and there was no fuel gauge until the 1960s.

1960s Splittie with larger rear window.

The Splittie became more practical as the camping conversions began to emerge. The 1960s improvements; the much larger (wider) rear window, introduced in August 1963; the 1500cc, 42bhp engine (available in the USA from January 1963 and universally across the range for the 1964 model year); and 12-volt electrics for the final year of production (August 1966), all serve to make a later Splittie an eminently practical classic. For would-be UK owners, consider one of the Australian imports that seem to be around nowadays. Rust free and RHD!

100%

August 1967 to July 1979 – Bay

Like the Splittie, the Bay also went

Early days Bay – rounded bumpers incorporating step.

1973 model and beyond – sturdier bumpers, repositioned indicators.

through a major facelift, in August 1972 (1973 model year). Successively larger engines offering more power helped the Bay to remain competitive (and become practical today). Initially, VW offered a 1584cc engine developing 47bhp and a maximum speed of 65mph. In 1970 (sadly at the expense of supreme reliability), the 1600 engine was modified (given twin-port cylinder heads), and power increased to 50bhp. This engine remained an option for most markets (not USA) throughout Bay production.

In August 1971, Bays came with a 1700, 66bhp engine, complete with twin carburettors, which gave a top speed of 76mph. In August 1973, the 1795cc unit added 2bhp. In August 1975, the 2-litre engine, producing 70bhp, was introduced. In the US, fuel injection replaced twin carburettors when the 1800 made its debut. Both twin carbs and fuel injection made home maintenance less easy.

In terms of value, a 2-litre Bay might have a slight advantage over an underpowered 1600 model. Body modifications (repositioned indicators,

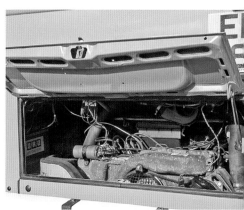

'76 onwards 2-litre engine – plenty of get up and go!

13

heftier bumpers, smaller VW logo at the front, which are the most noticeable aspects of the 1972 facelift), make not a jot of difference. Discs replaced drums up front in August 1970, and most owners preferred them! Auto box options, however, are another matter, at least in Europe. Expect to pay less for an auto-box, particularly on ready-to-use near Concours examples.

85%

Air-cooled T3 – 1600 or 2-litre engine 1979-1982.

August 1979 to July 1990 – The T3 (selected Syncro models to 1992)

Ten years ago, it appeared that values for the T3 would follow those of its predecessors in an upward spiral. Admittedly, there were those who would only consider the early air-cooled T3 models, but later Campers and Caravelles (the people carriers), endowed with reasonably powerful diesel engines, also had a following. The T3 club scene was strong and demand for the four-wheel-drive syncro models particularly so.

Ex-German services Kombi – often in excellent condition.

While it would be wrong to say that the club scene no longer exists and syncro models haven't got appeal, the T3 has been roundly eclipsed by later generations when it comes to both customising and desirability as a weekender or Camper. Despite near hyperinflation in relation to virtually all Splitties and most Bays, T3 prices have only shown at best a modest increase.

The most expensive models on the market today will be either a Camper in tip-top condition (whatever its age) and any vehicle with syncro. However, please don't regard the T3 as an investment.

45%

'89 model double cab Pickup Syncro T3.

Before you view
– be well informed

To avoid a wasted journey, and the disappointment of finding that the Bus does not match your expectations, it will help if you're very clear about what questions you want to ask before you pick up the telephone. Some of these points might appear basic, but when you're excited about the prospect of buying your dream classic, it's amazing how some of the most obvious things slip the mind. Also, check the current values of the model you're interested in via specialist Volkswagen magazines (classic vehicle guides consistently undervalue the VW Bus).

Where is the Bus?
Is it going to be worth travelling to the next county/state, or even across a border? A Bus advertised locally, although it may not sound very interesting, can add greatly to your knowledge for very little effort, so make a visit – it might even be in better condition than you expect.

Dealer or private sale?
Establish early on if the Bus is being sold by its owner or by a trader. A private owner should have all the history, so don't be afraid to ask detailed questions. A dealer may have more limited knowledge of a Bus' history, but should have some documentation. A dealer may offer a warranty/guarantee (ask for a printed copy) and finance.

Cost of collection and delivery
A dealer may well be used to quoting for delivery by transporter. A private owner may agree to meet you halfway, but only agree to this after you've seen the Bus at the vendor's address to validate the documents. Conversely, you could meet halfway and agree the sale, but insist on meeting at the vendor's address for the hand over.

View – when and where?
It's always preferable to view at the vendor's home or business premises. In the case of a private sale, the Bus' documentation should tally with the vendor's name and address. Arrange to view only in daylight, and avoid a wet day. Most Buses look better in poor light or when wet.

Reason for sale?
Do make it one of the first questions. Why is the Bus being sold and how long has it been with the current owner? How many previous owners?

Left-hand drive to right-hand drive
Although some Buses on the market were originally prepared for another country, it's unusual to find one that has been switched from LHD to RHD (common sense

would suggest steering clear of such vehicles unless, of course, they're late model Brazilian Bays specifically imported and converted by professional bodies). Generally, steering conversions can only reduce the value.

Condition (body/chassis/interior/mechanicals)
Ask for an honest appraisal of the Bus' condition. Ask specifically about some of the check items described in the '15 minute evaluation' chapter.

All original specification
An original equipment Bus is usually of higher value than a customised version, but these days there are some really tasty and 'professionally' modified Splitties around which can be worth a lot of money. For non-Concours, would-be camper conversion owners, originality doesn't really matter, as long as what you go for is fit for your purpose.

Matching data/legal ownership
Do VIN, chassis, engine, and license plate numbers match the official registration document? Is the owner's name and address recorded in the official registration documents?

For those countries that require an annual roadworthiness test, does the Bus have a document showing it complies (an MoT certificate in the UK, which can be verified on 0845 600 5977)?

If a smog/emissions certificate is mandatory, does the Bus have one?

If required, does the Bus carry a current road fund license/license plate tag?

Does the vendor own the Bus outright? Money might be owed to a finance company or bank; the Bus could even be stolen. Several organisations will supply the data on ownership, based on the Bus' license plate number; for a fee. Such companies can often also tell you whether the vehicle has been 'written off' by an insurance company. In the UK, the following organisations can supply vehicle data:

HPI – 01722 422 422
AA – 0870 600 0836
DVLA – 0870 240 0010
RAC – 0870 533 3660

Other countries will have similar organisations.

Unleaded fuel
Owners of older Buses, particularly those built in the 1950s and '60s and originally designed to run on leaded fuel, might opt to buy an additive to protect their engines. Nowadays suppliers of cylinder heads invariably offer products compatible with the use of unleaded petrol and, whereas ten years ago it seemed timely to remind owners of later fuel injected models and catalytic converters that their vehicles must run on unleaded, virtually all owners would take this for granted.

Insurance

Check with your existing insurer before setting out, your current policy might not cover you to drive the Bus if you do purchase it. Ideally, longer term (in the UK) go for classic insurance (although you might not get away with this with a later model T3). Although there isn't a no-claims bonus to be had, the Bus is unlikely to be your only vehicle, the prices are reasonable and, above all, you've got an agreed value.

How you can pay?

While cash will undoubtedly be welcome by all private sellers, on-line banking facilitates offer easy bank-to-bank transfers at the point of sale, assuming usage of a mobile device. Cheques (checks) are generally regarded as outmoded these days and a vendor will always be wary as they obviously take several days to clear.

Buying at auction?

If the intention is to buy at auction, see the 'Auctions' chapter for further advice.

Professional vehicle check (mechanical examination)

There are often marque/model specialists who will undertake professional examination of a vehicle on your behalf. Owners' clubs will be able to put you in touch with such specialists.

   Other organisations that will carry out a general professional check in the UK are:
AA – 0800 085 3007 (motoring organisation with vehicle inspectors)
ABS – 0800 358 5855 (specialist vehicle inspection company)
RAC – 0870 533 3660 (motoring organisation with vehicle inspectors)

Other countries will have similar organisations.

Inspection equipment

– these items will really help

This book
Reading glasses (if you need them for close work)
Magnet (not powerful, a fridge magnet is ideal)
Torch
Probe (a small screwdriver works very well)
Overalls
Mirror on a stick
Digital camera
A friend, preferably a knowledgeable enthusiast

Before you rush out of the door, gather together a few items that will help as you work your way around the proposed purchase. This book is designed to be your guide at every step, so take it along and use the check boxes to help you assess each area of the Bus you're interested in. Don't be afraid to let the seller see you using it.

Take your reading glasses if you need them to read documents and make close up inspections.

A magnet will help you check if the Bus is full of filler, although even a light skim can be dangerous in the long-term. Use the magnet to sample bodywork areas all around the Bus, particularly the lower sections, but be careful not to damage the paintwork. Ideally, there won't be any filler, but you might find a little here and there, but hopefully not whole panels.

A torch with fresh batteries will be useful for peering behind the wheels and under the Bus. It might even be useful in the engine compartment.

A small screwdriver can be used – with care – as a probe, particularly under the wheelarches and on the underside. With this you should be able to check an area for severe corrosion, but be careful – if it's really bad the screwdriver might go right through the metal! Get permission before you probe and, if it isn't granted and there's no explanation, walk away.

Be prepared to get dirty. Take along a pair of overalls, if you have them. Fixing a mirror at an angle on the end of a stick may seem odd, but with Bus cross-members and out-riggers this can be useful, even if you take our advice and crawl right under the Bus to see for yourself. A mirror will also help you to peer into the few crevices on a Bus.

Make sure that you take either a camera or your mobile (or other device) along with you so that you can study some areas of the Bus more closely later. Take a picture of any part of the Bus that causes you concern, and seek a friend's opinion.

Ideally, have a friend or knowledgeable enthusiast accompany you: a second opinion is always valuable.

Fifteen minute evaluation
– walk away or stay?

Exterior

When looking for a Bus, it's important not to buy the first one you see. Take your time and consider carefully the points in this book. Paint and bodywork are the most expensive to repair, due to the labour intensive nature of the procedures involved. With that in mind, you should think to yourself, 'how much of this could I do myself and how much do I need to farm out to someone with more expertise?' So, when you arrive at the vendor's home and, on the drive is this apparently immaculate Bus, stop, and remember what you've just read!

Lift the cab mats between seat and door to reveal rust.

On all the VW Buses one of the most vulnerable rust points is the front wheelarch and cab step. Check this by opening the front doors and having a good look around, lifting the cab mats between seat and door. The rear of the front wheelarch is another area that requires closer inspection. If this is flat metal, then it's been fitted with a repair panel (the original has flanges protruding which line up with the inner sills).

The battery is situated in the right-hand side of the engine bay of Splitties, Bays, and the T3 Diesel, with the common result that corrosion of the battery tray often results in rust appearing through the outer bodywork. The battery on other models of T3 is located under the right-hand front seat; this also needs checking for corrosion. Leisure batteries are often fitted under the left-hand front seat on T3 campers.

Rust in panel behind the front wheel revealing problems in sill and under floor areas.

The outline of the rear wheelarch can often be traced from the outside of the Bus due to corrosion of the welded seam. The body panels surrounding the engine are also vulnerable.

The lower edge of the front window frame of the Bay is prone to corrosion due to the design allowing water to accumulate under the rubber window surround. The front panel on all models should be checked for any damage over and above the usual stone chips. Body seams on T3s appear more prone to corrosion than those on earlier models.

The chassis is a fairly robust affair, but the outriggers can rust towards the outer ends. Bays after 1973 have a lower chassis plate covering the outriggers, which helps to keep the corrosion out. Rotten lower chassis plates, however, could imply problems with the outriggers and inner sills.

When the battery causes a hole in this panel the battery tray will be beyond redemption.

The front torsion bar tubes do rust, so they must be checked carefully, particularly where the outer uprights join the tubes. Rusty torsion bar tubes are an MoT failure point.

Outline of rear wheelarch can often be traced due to rust in the seam.

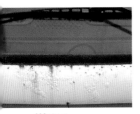

Water accumulating under window rubber surround causes corrosion in front panel.

Body seams, especially around petrol cap, prone to rust on T3s.

Interior

With three generations to cover in very few words, here's a summary! Ripped, stained or generally worn out seats and covers will cost more to replace the older the vehicle is. Replacement covers are available for most Splitties and Bays, although a visit to a scrapyard might be a cheaper option for a T3. Ripped or rotted headlinings are costly to replace via a professional, or tiresome to tackle yourself. The more basic the vehicle the more painted metal there will be.

Fittings, handles, knobs and switches tend to be better made and more robust the older the vehicle (also applicable to Camper conversions). Keep an eye open for T3 'gimmicks' that fall off in the hand. With regard to dashboards, look for evidence of tampering to fit modern stereos, and holes for extra switches. These are tiresome to rectify.

Furniture and cookers situated immediately behind the cab seats often hide rust, which often starts as a hole in the upright panel behind the front wheel.

Turning to the floor, lift up rubber mats or look for watermark stains on carpets. If there's evidence of water swilling about, or worse still the dreaded tin worm in action, unless it's a rare beast, bargain hard or avoid! Refer to 60 minute evaluation if any of the above is obvious.

Mechanicals

Most suspension components are readily available and affordable, except in the case of early Splitties, where the supply of new, old stock components is drying up. For example a 1950s track rod of the type fitted with grease nipples on the ball joints are very difficult to find. An exception to the 'readily available rule' is torsion bar tubes, which are prone to rusting where they join the upright shock absorber mounts. These should be checked carefully for corrosion, as they are relatively expensive and difficult to find (you might come across a used example from a Bus of similar vintage).

Vinyl seats split with age and the older the vehicle the more costly they can be to replace.

Furniture behind front seat of Bay often hides hole from interior to front wheelarch.

Next, look under the engine cover of a Split or Bay. Can you see the road through, or around, the black tinware around the rear of the Bus? (Note – when the rear of the engine is mentioned, it's the part that faces the rear of the car). The rubber seals around the engine tinware, along with the seals surrounding the tubing, play an important role in preventing overheating. If they are missing, the heat from the exhaust system is drawn into the engine fan, which is then used to cool the cylinders and heads, resulting in the engine 'frying' itself. Bays have a foam surround between the engine and

Splittie engine showing removable rear valance.

tinware, so it's advisable to check this thoroughly, as it has been known to break loose and be drawn into the fan, causing overheating and trashed engines.

Post-1963 air-cooled Buses are fitted with heat exchangers which are connected to the fan housing with black corrugated hoses (unless someone has fitted non-standard aluminium hoses, which deteriorate rapidly and look horrible!). These hoses, or the seals around them, are often missing, along with the pre-heat tube that supplies the carburettor with warm air. This is the third tube you should be able to see and it should be connected to a metal tube under the rear tinware, adjacent to the exhaust system. Some Buses from the late 1960s have smaller diameter tubing, which sometimes exits into the heat exchanger via the front engine plate.

Are the seals around the sparkplug connectors, which press into the cylinder surrounds, present, and making an airtight seal? If they're missing or broken, valuable cooling air is lost into the engine bay.

With the engine switched off and the keys away from the ignition, firmly grip the crankshaft pulley that drives the fan belt and attempt to push and pull it. If it moves visibly, the engine is nearing its last gasp, due to excessive wear on the front main bearing being beyond normal tolerances (0.004in or 0.01mm).

Next, have a look for oil leaks. A dribble of oil on one of the strainer plate studs isn't a problem, but lots of oil running down from higher up the engine and dripping off each sump cooling fin, could prove to be expensive.

Get the vendor to start the Bus while you watch the exhaust. A little smoke is normal, especially if the Bus is parked at a sideways tilt. The engine should settle down to a nice even tick-over with no smoke. A Bus built after June 1960 has an automatic choke, which turns off after two to three minutes. The engine should keep running when the choke turns off. However, late model Bays with badly worn carburettors, or leaking joints on the three-piece inlet manifold, may stall, or be stubborn about running sweetly until the engine is at optimum temperature.

Are there any knocking noises when the engine speed increases? This could be due to a variety of reasons, all of which could spell trouble in the future. Ignore slight tappet noises, as a loose tappet is better than a tight, very quiet one on a VW engine.

T3 engines are fitted with hydraulic tappets which, in the case of the 1600 CT series engine, can make a considerable clatter for several minutes after the engine is started.

Key points
– where to look for problems

All models are vulnerable around the cab step area. Look for rust on door bottoms, rust following outline of the rear wheelarches and seams on T3s. Check window seals, wheels, tyres and around the petrol filler (on T3s). Look at the right rear quarter-panel for evidence of corrosion due to battery acid. Campers – check for 'tatty' fabric on roof bellows.

Stone chip damage on all models, particularly Splitties and Bays. Rust around Bay headlamps and under the

windscreen, as well as the horizontal panel behind the bumper on T3s. Check under the front of the T3 for the spare wheel.

Check the engine for the presence of tinware, hoses, rubber seals and ancillaries. Pay particular attention to the condition of the foam seal on

all post-1973 Bay engines. Examine the engine and its surroundings for evidence of excessive amounts of sprayed oil. Pay particular attention to engine wiring. Check that the installed engine is correct for the model.

Check the engine lid hinges on post-1955 Splitties and all Bays. 1973 model Bays and later, including T3s – check for rusting seams on fixed rear valance. Check for rotten exhausts and heat exchangers on all air-cooled models.

Check head-linings and seats for stains and tears, plus rubber cab mats for wear. Check under carpets for damp, and carefully examine Camper interiors. The battery on petrol T3 models "lives" under the front seats.

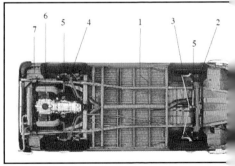

Check all points indicated. 1. Chassis and outriggers. 2. Torsion bars and uprights, Splitties and Bays. 3. Steering components. 4. Driveshaft joints and gaiters, reduction box housing on Splitties. 5. Shock absorbers, all models, coil springs, T3. 6. Engine oil leaks. 7. Battery tray, most models.

Serious evaluation

– 60 minutes for years of enjoyment

Circle the Excellent, Good, Average or Poor box of each section as you go along. The totting up procedure is detailed at the end of the chapter. Be realistic in your marking!

Exterior

Paint

Ex 4   Gd 3   Av 2   Pr 1

With all the generations under discussion dating from 1990 (1992) or earlier, the vast majority won't exhibit original, factory-applied paint. If you're aiming for Concours standards, it's important that the vehicle has a high quality paint finish, correct to the year it was manufactured. If you're lucky, you might find a silver sticker with black lettering indicating both VW's colour terminology and the code. A change of colour, if detected, will mean a loss of points. For Camper owners, well looked-after glossy paint is more important than genuine VW colours, although a pink Splittie may take some selling!

Once into re-sprays there are a number of points to look out for. Does the paintwork look like the skin of an orange? Are there obvious signs of runs? Is the paintwork flat, even though there are obvious traces of a recent application of polish? These are all signs that the work hasn't been done very well.

Be very wary of a Bus that has just come out of the paint-shop, as some vendors will see a way of making a quick profit by spending a little time and money hiding a myriad of horrors. This is where that magnet might come in handy, for if glossy hues hide filler and fibreglass, which, in turn, might mask lumps of the local newspaper, you'll have more than a hint of foul play when the magnet doesn't attract metal!

Finally, if you come across a Bus with old but original flat and faded paint, which nevertheless appears solid, don't dismiss it out of hand. It's amazing what a good application of 'T-cut' and polish can do.

Panels

Ex 4   Gd 3   Av 2   Pr 1

It's unusual to find much wrong with the roof of a Bus, the exception being basket case Splitties, which often rot all around the edges. Most vulnerable are the 'gutters' around the roof panel. Check the seam, where the gutter is folded back onto the main panel, for creeping surface rust, and, more importantly, look for crumbling gutters.

Panels around side windows are generally robust, particularly on Bays and Splitties, though the T3 is often rusty in this area.

The vulnerable part of the doors is the base, as drainage holes can become blocked allowing water to build up and rust to form. If the Bus is perfect apart from a door, don't panic, as reasonably-priced replacements are available for most years.

The hinges above the engine compartment lids on Bays and Splitties are vulnerable to rust: their prominent position being exposed to the elements (Barn door Splitties have a

Panels around side windows are susceptible to rust creeping from under the rubber window moulding.

Doors rust around the bottom due to blocked drainage holes.

A hole appearing above the bumper in the right-hand rear quarter indicates problems with the battery tray.

Access to the engine in T3 is different to Bays and Splitties. A small opening panel behind the number plate allows you to check water and oil levels.

sheltered piano hinge arrangement for the tailgate).

While at the back of a Splittie or a Bay it's worth checking the battery tray, situated to the right of the engine. The corrosive battery acid often rots the tray, and may also affect the rear right-hand quarter-panel.

The rear valance panel is removable on Splitties and pre-1973 Bays, which makes engine removal easy. Later Bays had a fixed valance, which is prone to rust in the seam joining it to the rear quarter-panel. The T3 has a small opening panel hidden by the rear number plate for checking the oil and, if applicable, water levels, with a removable engine inspection hatch only accessible once the tailgate has been lifted. T3 Pickups have an engine access hatch in the flatbed, as well as a tailgate-style opening rear engine cover.

The front panel, especially on Bays and Splitties, is extremely vulnerable to stone chips, causing considerable rusting if not treated. T3s, while having less painted metal on the front to rust, can have problems with the horizontal panel situated behind the front bumper, as water cannot drain away freely from this area.

Although the sills are not considered structural for MoT purposes, they are often rusty due to a serious deterioration in the vulnerable vertical panel behind the front wheel. This also has implications for the under-body protection plates, as well as the inner and outer sills. Pay particular attention to the lower sliding door channel in the sills on Bays and T3s, as rust here can cause the side door to fall off.

Pickup also has hatch in loading area to access ancillaries if you have long enough arms.

Due to their exposed position, engine lid hinges often rust.

Bays built in 1973 and after have a fixed rear valance – prone to rust in the seam joining it to rear quarterpanel.

Tailgate engine hatch is unique to the T3 Pickup.

Serious deterioration in the vulnerable panel behind the front wheel can be costly to rectify.

T3 panel joins are prone to rusting due to perished seam sealer allowing the ingress of water.

Splitties and Bays are vulnerable to front panel damage caused by stone chips.

Visible outline of inner rear wheelarch indicates costly corrosion where it joins the outer panel.

Recess behind front bumper on T3 is a water trap and can be rotten as a result.

As for the side panels, Splitties and Bays are relatively trouble-free, except around the outline of the rear wheelarch where it joins the side panel.

T3s tend to rust around all the panel joins, due to the sealer used in the manufacturing process becoming hardened with age and cracking, in turn allowing water ingress on unprotected

Metal and panel joints around petrol cap on T3s can rust as spilt fuel removes protective polish and hastens demise of seam sealer.

metal within the seam. The fuel filler cap on a T3 is situated just behind the right-hand front door, and the metal around it often rusts due to spilt fuel removing protective polish.

Other Bus rust points

Check the front wheelarches, paying particular attention to the cab step and under the mats adjacent to the cab seats. The mats often conceal rust on an otherwise respectable Bus. The whole front cab area is vulnerable to the dreaded tin worm, so check where the floor joins the front panel; look long and hard at the torsion bar tubes on Bays and Splitties; and also the front chassis rails and suspension

Pay particular attention to the cab step and wheelarch area, both of which are prone to rust.

Damaged trim on Sambas can be reasonably costly to replace, as can the shiny VW emblem.

mounting points on all Buses. Poking and probing here is important, as chassis rails are likely to be expensive if extensive welding is necessary, while torsion bar tubes should not be welded and are expensive to replace. If the Bus has already been welded, make sure the job has been competently executed. Be suspicious if a recent concrete-like coat of underseal has been plastered on!

Lifting the mat over the top of the wheelarch can sometimes reveal a lot of rust.

Shut lines

Doors do drop with heavy usage, neglect, and age. Check that the cab door doesn't drop when opened (scraping the step of earlier Bays in the process).

Exterior trim

Even the more elaborate incarnations of the Splittie and Bay lacked much trim. Chrome was more or less restricted to some headlamp surrounds and most handles, but by the mid-1970s, Volkswagen was downgrading to plastic wherever it could. Microbus Deluxe anodised side strips are reasonably costly to replace, but 'name badges' were made in more durable materials. The VW symbol on the front of Splitties and Bays, when not painted, is also reasonably easy and not too expensive to replace. Hubcaps, until the plastic T3 era, were usually painted and replacements can easily be bought (chrome ones too). Chromed Bay bumpers also tend to be fairly long lasting.

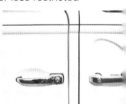

Door handles on Splitties and Bays are robust. Perhaps T3 ones, which incorporate plastic, won't stand the test of time quite so well.

By the time of the T3, an era of trim austerity had infected motor manufacturers generally, and even upmarket T3s began to feature moulded plastic bumpers/spoilers.

The 'church-key' – a feature of Splitties from March 1955 to August 1965 – opens the petrol flap and the engine lid, and is stored on a bracket in the

Wipers

A great variety of wiper blades and arms have been produced over the years. Early Splittie options might prove tricky

Splittie wiper blades are more difficult and costly to replace than later Bays and T3s, which are much more like the modern car ones of today.

to locate, and will be expensive, though. There should be no problems either on price or availability with all Bay and T3 options.

Sunroof and elevating tops

Ex	Gd	Av	Po
4	3	2	1

All opening/elevating tops are prone to leaks and need to be checked. A Splittie fold-back canvas roof will be easier to deal with than a metal wind-back Bay version. Leaking Camper roofs are not only tiresome, but invariably costly to replace, if the 'parts' can be found.

Canvas roofs – though not cheap to replace – are easier to cope with than a leaking metal sunroof. Plexiglass roof lights are unique to Sambas.

Glass

Ex	Gd	Av	Po
4	3	2	1

Glass for most ages of Bus is fairly readily available, though it's unusual to find a Bus that actually needs replacement windows. Keep an eye out for non-original windows in homespun camper conversions, where bleary, scratched Perspex may have been fitted. Also, remember that the Samba had Plexiglass (similar to Perspex) roof lights, the same material being used for the wraparound window in each rear quarter (until the 1964 model year).

Lights

Ex	Gd	Av	Po
4	3	2	1

Until August 1966 and the 1967 model year, all Splitties 'suffered' from six-volt electrics. Tarnished or rusted reflectors in any age of headlamp will result in roadworthiness test failures, but replacements are readily available for just about every age. The location of the headlamp on a Bay means that rust can form below the unit.

There's a plethora of early rear light housings, most of which can be replaced through specialists or at shows (but will command premium prices). The more modern the van, the more plastic dominates.

Second-hand units for the T3 tend to be relatively inexpensive.

Check that semaphore indicators are in good condition on vehicles so fitted,

Bullet indicators were introduced in the USA in 1955, and in Europe in 1960.

Camper elevating roofs are always prone to leaks. British 'Devon' conversions with vertically elevating tops are amongst the worst offenders.

as replacements will be costly. Many enthusiasts have added aftermarket indicators to make their vans safer. Most Concours judges will turn a blind eye to this, unless the unit fitted is particularly obnoxious. Auxiliary lights fitted to both Bays and T3s will result in points being deducted, but if camping is your choice, and you're happy with the aesthetics, don't worry.

The so-called 'fish-eye' indicator appeared in 1961 in the USA and in 1963 for other markets.

Between 1961 and August 1971 European Splitties and Bays had this style of segmented rear lights with amber indicator section.

Wheels and tyres

All buses were fitted with cross-ply tyres until July 1967. From that point only the Microbus L benefited from radials; that is, until August 1971 when the rest followed suit (except for some 1600 models). Today, it's logical to fit radials, unless adherence to the feel of the period when the Bus was built is paramount to a Concours entrant. Wheels were five-stud until the end of production, and painted white until August 1970 when silver became the order of the day. Hubcaps were domed until the same point, and eventually disappeared in favour of either plastic discs or alloy wheels.

From August 1970, when disc brakes arrived, wheels contained round ventilation holes.

Splitties had three progressively smaller sizes of wheels. This model dating from 1964 or later has 14in wheels, the smallest option. All Splitties and early Bays had domed hubcaps.

Types of wheel

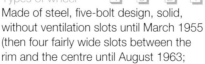

Made of steel, five-bolt design, solid, without ventilation slots until March 1955 (then four fairly wide slots between the rim and the centre until August 1963; narrower slots after this). Originally 16in diameter, reduced to 15in in March 1955, and to 14in in August 1963. Originally 5.50 x 16 tyres; from March 1955 – 6.40 x 15, and 7.00 x 14 from August 1963. Bay wheels were 5J x 14 until August 1970, 5½J x 14 thereon, with circular

After the introduction of disc brakes in August 1970, wheel rims contained ventilation holes and had flatter hubcaps fitted.

ventilation holes replacing narrow slots. 185 x 14 radials were fitted to the Microbus L, from the arrival of the new Bay model, and on all other larger-engined models from August 1970. When launched, T3 wheels were of the same design as those on the Bay.

Alloy wheels first appeared on the Caravelle Carat in late 1983. A 16in wheel option became available from September 1986 on Syncro models. From 1987, 205/70 tyres were fitted on the Caravelle Coach (1987), and on the Caravelle GL from September 1989.

Check that the Bus has the wheels Volkswagen intended, if that's what you really want. Check the wheels for damage. Buckled rims may mean that the Bus has hit the kerb which, in turn, could have damaged suspension components. Are the wheels rusty, or is there evidence of the wheels having been re-painted? Bus wheels are notorious for rust damage, and badly pitted ones are difficult to restore to factory standard. Kerbed alloys will always be unsightly.

Tyres

Check that the tyres are all the same type. A mix and match of makes will lose points in any Concours and isn't ideal elsewhere. Crucially, ensure that there isn't a lethal mixture of radial and crossply tyres on offer as, apart from anything else, it's illegal!

Hub bearings and steering joints, steering box/rack
With the front of the Bus safely supported on axle stands, spin the wheels. Hub bearings are usually noisy if worn out. To check for play in the bearings, grip the wheel at the top and bottom and rock it. If there is play, but the bearings weren't noisy, the problem is minor, and an adjustment can be easily made. However, if play is present but it's not the wheel bearings, then this could prove more expensive, as the wear is in the king and/or link pins on Splitties, or the stub axle swivel joints on later models. On T3s, this type of play could be in the various suspension wishbone joints. Check that the ball joints on the track rods are free of excessive play (MoT

Beetle kingpin and linkpin front stub axle, Splitties very similar.

Look for rust in torsion bar uprights on Bays and check play in steering swivel ball joints.

T3 uses coil spring suspension – check for play in all joints and bushes.

stations use a pry bar to check the condition of the various ball joints, so if you are in any doubt, it might be prudent to enlist the help of your friendly tester).

With the steering in the straight-ahead position, turn the steering wheel left and right. There should be no more than 1 inch of movement before the wheels start to move. More than this amount is indicative of a steering box that needs adjustment or, in extreme cases, replacing. Models with steering racks should have very little play.

Interior
Seats

4 3 2 1

Unlike some of the earliest Beetles, where cloth was used to cover the seats, all Buses were decked out in vinyl. Inevitably, for the Panelvan, seating was restricted

to the cab, and, until 1963, even the more luxurious models suffered from a single, three-person, non-adjustable bench. The norm in material in the early days was a fine-grained grey/black vinyl. Padding was slightly more generous on the Kombi's rear seats, while those on the Microbus models were both pleated and piped. As the years went by, slightly more elaborate patterns emerged, particularly for vehicles other than the Panelvan and Pickup.

Inevitably, vinyl will have split and cracked with age, while 'trim' like piping is particularly vulnerable. Replacement material is available for just about every Bus, though the more ornate or complex the trim and design, the more difficult it will be to match perfectly. Although firms converting Buses into Campers tended to look more at head-linings and carpets in their packages, some seats were re-covered and, in later years, owners might also have upgraded to cloth. From a non-Concours, happy camper buying point of view, well-preserved frames and springs are more important than the covering.

Bay models and many T3s persisted with practical vinyl, varying from a simple

Vinyl seats split with age and wear.

T3 interiors became increasingly sumptuous with top of the range models even featuring armrests. Watch out for torn/bleached or cigarette burnt upholstery.

Splittie Kombis were basic
– no door cards
– definitely no carpet, and ...

... wing nuts released the seats, while rubber matting added to the austere nature of the interior.

basket weave design up to air permeable covers, and combining more than one colour and texture of vinyl. Although of the same basic design, seats in the Bay and the T3 were heftier and generally better shaped than the Splittie offering. Although all materials are particularly hardwearing, in the event of damage, replacement covers are available. More luxurious and later T3s were decked out with cloth upholstery, ranging from relatively hardwearing tweed effect material, to sumptuous, but susceptible, velour. Check out all cloth upholstery for sun damage (rot and fading), tears, and difficult to shift stains. US Bays, and the more luxurious T3s for all markets might have headrests, so make sure that any moveable parts function properly.

Carpets 4 3 2 1

You can forget about carpet, at least until you encounter a Caravelle-type T3. VW offered instead practical, hardwearing rubber matting in all cabs and in the rear compartment of passenger carrying Buses. Only the Microbus Deluxe (or 'L' in the Bay era) featured any carpet, and this was restricted to the rear luggage compartment over the engine. Rubber matting can usually be replaced if it's worn, but always make a point of lifting what you can, to see whether water is swilling about or, worse still, the tin worm has already taken hold.

Campers of all ages are likely to feature carpet or non-standard coverings, at least in the main body of the Bus (small lino tiles were a favourite of converters working on Splitties). The only real message is to treat these like VW's offerings, and lift where you can to see if any horrors lurk beneath. T3s, readily supplied with carpets, are really like any modern car. Beware worn foot-well carpet that hasn't been protected by a mat, and be suspicious if any area is either wet, or shows signs of water staining.

Bay rubber matting in the cab area (note the quirky, jointed handbrake).

Head-lining 4 3 2 1

In Splittie days, Panelvans, Pickups and Kombis had plain hardboard head-linings in the cab and bare metal where applicable in the rear. Until September 1964, both versions of Microbus had a full-length cloth head-lining, and these are the ones that are highly likely to have rotted, or been ripped, over the years. Replacement material is available but can be difficult to fit. From September 1964, white vinyl with a myriad of tiny perforations became standard. With the arrival of the Bay, even the Panelvan and Pickup acquired a vinyl head-lining in the cab. Vinyl remained the order of the day well into the T3 era, although later models lost their little perforations. Vinyl head-linings are susceptible to careless characters causing tears and rips. They can also be difficult to clean where a persistent smoker has been the owner. Campers inevitably have all sorts of different head-linings: some roof panels are even partially carpeted. Check for signs of water staining, particularly where a pop-top is fitted.

Door cards

From simple fibreboard in the cab only, to dual-tone, colour-coded vinyl and moulded plastic fitments, wherever a door card is fitted, check to see if it has warped. Apart from the hassle of replacing it, which can be something of problem in Splittie 'barn door' terms, warped door cards can spell trouble in other respects, as they are a reliable sign of water ingress and subsequent blockages.

Door cards in upmarket Splittie models were often two-tone to match the external paint colours. If damaged, they can be difficult to replace.

Door locks

4 3 2 1

In a word, robust, although any dodgy character intent on breaking into a Bus would have little trouble, as all were designed in an age when lowlife hadn't cottoned on to 'borrowing' Buses to a significant extent. Locks varied in design considerably over the years.

Door buttons, on Bays, etc, a nuisance if not intact.

Door handles

4 3 2 1

Externally prone to corrosion if not cared for, although plastics started to emerge as the Bay ebbed. VW's internal door handles ranged from well-made chrome fitments, to a series of plastic door pulls. Whatever the age of the Bus, it's fairly unusual to encounter damage, and replacements can be picked up.

Window winders

4 3 2 1

Splittie cab side windows slide; Bays and T3s wind. While apparently robust in operation, the use of plastic-based winder mechanisms has made them susceptible to failure in later years. Check that the window winder isn't too stiff in operation, and doesn't creak and groan as it carries out its job. Either way, it's a sign that the mechanism contained within the door panel is on its way out, something that will eventually lead to the winder giving up the ghost. Also check later quarter-light catches. When VW became security conscious and fitted chunkier and, allegedly, thief-proof catches (we are talking Bay models here), it also created something that was more prone to failure. In the modern style, you'll be lucky to find a T3 with quarter-lights.

Steering wheel

4 3 2 1

All Bus steering wheels are larger than their equivalents in VW passenger cars. Three-spoke until March 1955, and black for all models except the Microbus Deluxe, which luxuriated in an ivory offering. For the rest of Splittie production, a two-spoke item, again in black and ivory was on offer. Bay steering wheels were black and two-spoke, becoming larger with wider spokes in 1977. At launch, the

Splittie dashes were all-metal affairs throughout the production run. Two-spoke steering wheel denotes a post March '55 model.

Bay dash – steering wheel with control stalks for lights and indicators and dash insert for three gauges.

T3s steering wheel was perceived to have lost style, but remained a two-spoke item and was comfortable enough to use. Except for Splitties, the steering wheel is unlikely to need any form of renovation. For older models, there are a number of firms which can refurbish your existing ivory wheel, and others who can sell you a replacement.

Splittie speedo is very basic, with just three additional warning lights.

T3 dash – more controls giving car-like feel.

Instrument panel

Ex	Cd	Av	Po
4	3	2	1

There were basically four offerings: pre-1955 single dial binnacle (except Microbus Deluxe); metal full length dash for post-1955 Splitties; plastic and finished in black to prevent reflections, but still fairly austere, for the Bay; and an item that would be more or less at home in a car for the T3. Remember that there was no fuel gauge for the Splittie until 1961. Period accessories like clocks and radios are worth quite a lot. Inevitably, where padded vinyl is involved, there is a risk of splitting due to the action of the sun. Watch out for the more flimsy car-style fittings of the eighties – as we all know, these can easily break or crack. Also beware modern in-car entertainment installations, as these can often mean damage to the original panel (as well as holes in door cards).

Handbrake

Ex	Cd	Av	Po
4	3	2	1

All Buses have a handbrake with separate cables to each rear wheel. If adjusted correctly, it should operate with a maximum of seven clicks.

Spare wheel well

Ex	Cd	Av	Po
4	3	2	1

Early Splitties had their spare wheel located within the engine compartment. When the design of the rear changed for the 1955

Bay, brake master-cylinder reservoir hides under the driver's seat controls.

model to separate doors for interior and engine, it became necessary to relocate the spare wheel to a compartment behind the cab seats. This area rarely gives trouble unless the spare wheel has been put away wet.

Lift out the spare wheel from its position just inside the tailgate on the left side of a Bay Bus, and thoroughly check the well. This is not usually a problem area, but is still worth checking. T3s have their spare wheel situated in a drop down carriage forward of the front axle and this should be checked for ease of use.

Useful toolkit and spare bulb set for a Splittie.

Jack and tool kit

The tool kit in a Bay is a simple collection of the basics and should be stored in a leatherette bag under the left front seat. While elsewhere we have advocated the jack's use only in a dire emergency, it should, nevertheless, be present.

Putting the spare wheel away wet caused the well on this Bay to rust. Note the safety strap for securing the wheel.

Body jack and wheel wrench for a Bay stored in a vinyl bag under front passenger seat.

Mechanicals
Under the bonnet – general impression

Go to the back and lift the engine lid. Is it beautifully clean with everything in place? If the answer is yes, the chances are that it's been well looked after. If you find it covered in oil, plus a black film on the inside of the engine lid, then it's probably been thrashed. There's even the possibility of a broken ring or burnt piston.

Although you should have made this check during the 15-minute evaluation, it's worth repeating. With the engine switched off, grip the crankshaft pulley and rock it fore and aft. The movement should be barely perceptible (0.004in/0.01mm). More than this, and the engine has been through the wars and is probably in need of a rebuild.

Is the generator/cooling fan drive belt adjusted to the correct tension? If not, then chances are it's been slipping, with a resulting loss of cooling air to the engine. This can have serious implications for an air-cooled engine, such as cracked cylinder heads, or cracked/broken pistons and rings. In recent years, there has been a tendency for owners to remove the thermostat and cooling control flaps from the bottom of the fan housing, in the mistaken belief that it will improve the cooling to the cylinders and heads. The angle of the flaps has been designed to direct most of the air to the hottest part of the engine, which is the cylinder head. The thermostat is there to allow the engine to warm up quickly to its most efficient temperature. To check if the thermostat is in place, look under the right-hand side of the engine between the crankcase and the heat exchanger or heater-box. On pre-1963 cars,

Simple 1500 engine – the most powerful supplied for a Splittie.

1600 twin-port Bay engine, still simple but more complex carburettor.

2-litre air-cooled T3 engine – sturdy but complicated by comparison.

the heater control will need to be in the off position, as this opens the rear flaps. On post-1963 cars, there's a two-piece section of tinware that, with the aid of a torch, you must look above, to find the thermostat.

In the 15-minute evaluation reference has already been made to the importance of the engine bay seals, including those around the air hoses, which should also be in good condition to prevent the loss of cooling air, not to mention precious heating air.

Chassis and engine numbers

Of the two, the chassis number is more important in determining the age of the Bus. Until 1980, when an international standardised numbering system applied to all vehicle manufacturers, VW's system was relatively straightforward.

Splitties: The last Splittie produced in a given calendar year would bear the following number:
1950 – 20-008112
1951 – 20-020112
1952 – 20-041857
1953 – 20-070431
1954 – 20-110603
1955 – 20-160735
1956 – 223 216
1957 – 315 209
1958 – 416 082

Bay chassis number is in the engine compartment. Note the foam engine surround.

1959 – 546 843
1960 – 710 069
1961 – 882 314
1962 – 1 047 967
1963 – 1 222 500
1964 – 215 082 480
The new numbering system was as follows: the first two digits indicate the Bus type (21 equals Panelvan, for example), the third digit represents the model year:
1965 – 216 083 207
1966 – 217 079 889
1967 (end of July) 217 148 459

Bays: Throughout the Bay's run, model years were more important than calendar years. The following table shows the first and last chassis numbers as recorded by Volkswagen for each given year. Note: 21 denotes the Panelvan. Other options include: 22 – Microbus, 23 – Kombi, Microbus Deluxe – 24, Pickup – 26.
1968 MY: August 1st 1967 – 218 000 001   – July 31st 1968 – 218 202 251
1969 MY: August 1st 1968 – 219 000 001   – July 31st 1969 – 219 238 131
1970 MY: August 1st 1969 – 210 000 0001 – July 31st 1970 – 210 2 248 837
1971 MY: August 1st 1970 – 211 2 000 001 – July 31st 1971 – 211 2 276 560
1972 MY: August 1st 1971 – 212 2 000 001 – July 31st 1972 – 212 2 246 946
1973 MY: August 1st 1972 – 213 2 000 001 – July 31st 1973 – 213 2 254 657
1974 MY: August 1st 1973 – 214 2 000 001 – July 31st 1974 – 214 2 194 943
1975 MY: August 1st 1974 – 215 2 000 001 – July 31st 1975 – 215 2 155 145
1976 MY: August 1st 1975 – 216 2 000 001 – July 31st 1976 – 216 2 300 000
1977 MY: August 1st 1976 – 217 2 000 001 – July 31st 1977 – 217 2 300 000
1978 MY: August 1st 1977 – 218 2 000 001 – July 31st 1978 – 218 2 300 000
1979 MY: August 1st 1978 – 219 2 000 001 – Oct 31st 1979 – 219 2 153 964

T3: From 1980, a standardised international chassis number system was used, which applied to all manufacturers. The 17 character chassis 'number' consists of a combination of numbers and letters, the first three of which identify the manufacturer and 'brand'. For the Bus this appears as 'WV2'. The next three characters are fill-ins, while characters 7 and 8 refer to the 'designation of type' (25). 9 is, again, a fill-in; 10 indicates the year of manufacture (1980 = A, 1981= B, etc) and 11 identifies the production factory (H = Hanover, for example). The remaining digits are serial numbers starting at 000 001 for each new model year.

Engine numbers are stamped on the block throughout. Providing the chassis number tallies with the vendor's documents, the rest is really academic (except for purist Concours entrants).

Wiring

Ex Gd Av Po
4 3 2 1

The bulk of the wiring will be visible under the dashboard. It's a fairly simple arrangement on early Splitties, with only four fuses in the front fuse box. Bizarrely, the two fuses for the main beam headlights are in the engine compartment, adjacent to the fuel tank. The rear fuse box had two more fuses added at a later date, to protect the dipped beam headlights. A front dash only fuse box containing six fuses superseded this. By the end of Splittie production the number of fuses had grown to eight, and 12-volt electrics were introduced in the final year.

The fuse and relay plate is under the dashboard of Bays and T3.

Are there lots of crimped insulated spade connectors with gaudy red, blue or yellow insulation? This usually indicates trouble, especially if accompanied by a rat's nest of non-standard wiring colours. Worse still, you may find tap connectors better known as 'Scotch-lock' connectors. These are great to get you home with a temporary repair, but invariably give trouble if used long term.

There are surprisingly few wires in the engine bay but, due to the heat and possible presence of oil, the insulation often becomes brittle. Particularly prone to this problem is the important wire from the oil pressure warning light switch. On Buses built during the 1960s and on, check that the black wire from the coil to the fuel cut-off valve via the auto-choke is present and in good condition. Early Buses have the voltage regulator mounted on the generator in the engine bay; later Buses have it mounted on the engine bulkhead. Make sure that the connections to the regulator are tight and corrosion free. Alternators fitted on later Bays and T3s usually have an integral voltage regulator.

Bays up to 1970 have a fuse box containing 10 fuses, whereas on later models there were 12 fuses, and the fuse box incorporated a self-contained relay console. All models up to 1972 have fairly simple wiring, illustrated in good workshop manuals with easy to read wiring diagrams. After 1972, however, wiring becomes more complex (and workshop manuals were illustrated with harder to follow current flow charts). By the time T3s arrived on the scene, the wiring looms were built following the modern practice of using multi-plugs to join the various systems. Although each connector has terminal numbers to enable you to trace circuits, they are much more complicated for the home restorer to follow if a fault occurs. However, if you're just dismantling a component to work on the bodywork, then it makes life simple, because you just have to disconnect a multi-plug.

Battery

On all models up to the end of Bay production in 1979, plus diesel T3s, the battery is mounted to the right of the engine within the engine compartment. Petrol-engined T3 batteries are located under the right-hand cab seat. If there is a lot of corrosion on the terminals, the battery is probably past its best. Beware the owner who charges the battery before you arrive!

The T3 battery is located under the driver's seat.

Washer system

Ex 4 Gd 3 Av 2 Po 1

Windscreen washers were factory-fitted from August 1960, and were operated by a push switch in the centre of the windscreen wiper switch. 1960 models were pressurised by a hand pump on the instrument panel. They were not factory-fitted to early Splitties and you are likely to find all manner of ingenious devices to comply with retrospective regulations introduced in the UK.

Bays have a washer bottle incorporating a tyre valve, which is usually pressurised at the same time as the tyres, and is actuated by a valve in the windscreen wiper stalk, situated on the right of the steering column. This system is very simple and only fails through loss of compressed air. The bottle holds about one litre and is situated behind the fibreboard panel in the front of the cab.

Screen washer bottle and 'top hat' cover behind the front panel under a Bay dash.

Engine leaks

Ex 4 Gd 3 Av 2 Po 1

Have a good look above and below the engine. Is it plastered with oil and muck? Remove the oil filler cap and check for a buff coloured, creamy gunge. Spilt oil at the top of the engine could be due to insufficient care being taken when topping up, or to the black tin surrounding the oil filler tube being either loose or rusted through (thanks to water in the aforementioned creamy gunge). It could also be a result of perished oil cooler seals, or worn pistons and piston rings (causing the crankcase to pressurise and oil to blow out of every available orifice).

Looking underneath, oil at the front of the engine, where it joins the transmission, is usually attributable to the crankshaft oil seal, although it could also be the gearbox shaft seal. Gearbox oil has a very strong smell.

Oil along the right-hand side of the engine is either from the valve cover gasket, or leaking push rod tube oil seals. Check this with a torch, looking above the tinware between the heat exchanger and the crankcase. Also, check in the same place on the right-hand side for the thermostat as this will often have been removed (a definite no-no). Examine the left-hand side for the same leaks, but also look above the pushrod tubes for the presence of oil. If you find oil here, suspect the oil cooler and/or push rod tube seals again, or the crankcase could be cracked (a terminal condition, requiring a complete engine rebuild using a replacement crankcase).

Engine and transmission mountings

Ex 4 Gd 3 Av 2 Po 1

Because the engine hangs from the rear of the gearbox on Splitties, there are no engine mountings as such. The gearbox is mounted between the rear floorpan forks on a metal cradle. You can check the rubber mountings between the cradle and the gearbox to see if they have been affected by oil. They rarely give any trouble but the rubber mount can sometimes separate from its metal backing plate. The third mounting point is at the front of the gearbox and, again, can only be visually inspected. This is best done with the Bus on a ramp, as you can then try to move the front of the gearbox up and down to check if the mount is sound.

The Bay employs a different setup, with a front gearbox mounting and a rear engine support bar suspended between the chassis members and bolted to the rear of the crankcase. The engine support bar on early Bays is of a welded pressed-steel construction and is prone to rot, causing the engine to drop. Later Bays have a solid bar to support the engine. Later Bays also have a rear transmission support bracket which, in turn, is suspended from a crossmember. This negates the need to support the gearbox when the engine is removed.

The T3 employs much the same method to support the engine and gearbox.

Intake manifold

The carburettor to inlet manifold gasket on pre-1971 engines, plus the metal ring between the manifold and the cylinder heads, should be in good condition to prevent air leaks. Air getting into the inlet manifold will cause a weakening of the fuel/air mixture. A hissing noise emanating from the manifold will indicate the problem.

The handlebar-type manifold used on pre-1971 engines rarely gives any trouble in itself, but the attached pre-heat pipe can rust through or become blocked with carbon. Check the pre-heat pipe and then, with the engine running, check if it warms up. Be very careful, as this pipe can get very hot if it's working correctly (as a precaution, check for warmth near the centre under the carburettor). A consequence of this pipe being blocked is that the upright part of the manifold can ice up during winter, causing rough running.

Post-1971 engines have twin port heads and a three-piece inlet manifold. Check the two rubber joints, held in place by hose clips, as these can perish and cause a weakening of the mixture.

Inlet manifold, showing carburettor 'hot spot' tube.

Bays produced for the European market, with the more robust 1700 to 2000cc engines, have a twin carburettor setup, and the manifolds are relatively troublefree.

Carburettors/fuel injection system

Early carburettors are less troublesome than those used on later Buses which, thanks to anti-pollution legislation, have been made more complicated. The main throttle spindle can get sloppy, however, causing air leaks and a small loss of fuel, the result of which will be poor running. Try to rock the spindle back and forth to check for this.

Due to wear and tear, a lot of Bus carburettors have been replaced. Consequently, it's not unusual to find a Bus fitted with a Weber carburettor, which is fine (except for finicky Concours judges). Sadly, others have copies of the original Solex from dubious origins, which can be troublesome, thanks to poor workmanship

2-litre T3 engine showing twin carburettors with air cleaner removed.

during manufacture. You may be able to locate a company rebuilding original Solex carbs, complete with new throttle spindle bearings, and these are a better bet. In the USA, some Bays with the 1800cc, and all 2000cc engines, came with electronic fuel injection. These are relatively trouble free, with any problems usually attributable to air leaks in the various hoses, or faults in the double relay situated near number 3 cylinder. It's also essential that the ignition and valve clearances are regularly serviced.

Exhaust

Ex	Gd	Av	Po
4	3	2	1

The best and most efficient exhaust systems are the type fitted by the factory. Many Buses have been fitted with go-faster aftermarket extractor systems in the vain hope of more power. These systems cause complications to the heating system of air-cooled models, as they lack the transfer pods for the heater tubes from the fan housing. Additionally, their pipework might be so close to the bodywork that it blisters the paint. 1700 to 2000cc air-cooled Buses have fewer problems with aftermarket exhaust systems, due to the different design of the heater system. However, they are still very noisy!

Exhaust systems on air-cooled models rarely last more than two years if the Bus is in continuous use. An exhaust is relatively cheap to buy if made by the original equipment manufacturer and then purchased from an independent trader. Inevitably, exhausts for 25/30bhp engines are more difficult to source and will cost more, but the fact that an otherwise excellent Bus has a 'dodgy' exhaust shouldn't deter a potential purchaser. Original exhausts usually fail near the seam on the end of the main box.

1700 Bay cylinder head and heat exchanger.

Heat exchanger used from 1963 on all engines up to 1600cc.

Gearbox, rear axle (transmission) and clutch

Ex	Gd	Av	Po
4	3	2	1

Bus transmissions, especially on early vehicles, are relatively trouble free, with even noisy examples going on for years before anything breaks. Sometimes, however, you will find one that slips out of gear, but this is rare. Noise in the transmission system usually comes from the final drive (crown wheel and pinion). The usual problems are driveshaft related, with the Splitties' swing axles having leaky driveshaft gaiters and worn out, or leaky, reduction boxes. The reduction boxes are fitted to the ends of the driveshafts and transfer the power from the axle shafts to the

The torsion bar sprung, double-jointed rear axle of a Bay.

T3 used coil springs with double-jointed rear axles.

rear stub axles. They serve to reduce the gearing and increase the ride height. The double-jointed driveshafts fitted to Bays and T3s suffer from worn constant velocity joints, or split joint gaiters. Check the swing axle gaiters, or constant velocity joint gaiters, for damage. Badly worn constant velocity joints click (mainly when cornering).

For the 1973 model year, automatic transmission became an option with the 1700cc engine. Be suspicious if an automatic Bus fails to reach top speed or accelerates poorly. This can be due to incorrect torque converter fluid levels, a faulty torque converter, or a major fault with the automatic gearbox. In 1985, permanent all-wheel drive Syncro versions of the T3 became available. It would be advisable to enlist the services of an expert to inspect either an automatic or Syncro Bus, as parts and labour are likely to be prohibitively expensive if you make a hasty decision and end up with a lemon.

On manual Buses, the clutch is checked for free play at the pedal and should be between 10-20mm.

Test drive (not less than 15 minutes)
Main warning lights (telltales)
There are two warning lights situated in the speedometer head that are important for the health of the engine: the red generator warning light, and the green oil pressure warning light. On some earlier models, and then again with later ones, both lights are red. When the engine starts both lights should extinguish. On Buses with very good oil pressure the green warning light may stay on for a few seconds after the engine is switched off as long as the ignition is still on. Remove the green wire from the coil to stop the engine if you want to check this.

Cold start
On Buses built before August 1959, pull out the manual choke, and with later models, press the accelerator pedal once to activate the automatic choke. Then, with your foot off the accelerator pedal, turn the starter key and the vehicle should start if it has been correctly maintained.

Operation clutch
The clutch pedal, which should have 10-to-20mm of free play before you can feel the spring pressure, can now be depressed and the gearlever should slip smoothly into first. On releasing the clutch it should not judder. A juddering clutch can be caused by three things: oil on the driven plate, not enough curve in the conduit between the chassis and the bracket on the gearbox, or being badly worn.

Operation gearbox (including reverse)
Splitties built before March 1953 were equipped with a crash box, which required

the driver to double de-clutch when changing gear. Until May 1959, when full synchromesh was introduced, only first gear was non-synchromesh. If the vehicle has been maintained properly, the synchromesh boxes fitted to Buses usually work with a very smooth action. When testing, drive the Bus fairly hard in each gear, making sure that it doesn't jump out of any them. Test reverse in the same way, somewhere quiet, like an empty car park. Find reverse by pushing down on the lever, which is then moved to the left and backwards.

Operation auto box
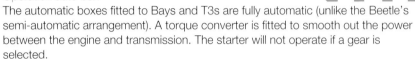

The automatic boxes fitted to Bays and T3s are fully automatic (unlike the Beetle's semi-automatic arrangement). A torque converter is fitted to smooth out the power between the engine and transmission. The starter will not operate if a gear is selected.

When testing, select 'drive' and accelerate through the 'gears'. Be suspicious of a faulty torque converter or forward clutch in the auto box if the Bus is sluggish or fails to reach top speed. Note the speeds when the gear changes take place. The changes should take place quickly without interrupting the power from the engine. If the engine races between gears then there may be trouble lurking within the box. Also check that the kick-down mechanism is working correctly.

Steering feel

Although heavy, when compared to modern power-assisted vehicles (European T3 Carat models had power steering, as did many later US Vanagons), the steering should feel light and positive once on the move. The general tendency is towards oversteer and the most stable technique is to approach a bend at a speed where you can gently accelerate through it.

Lowered Buses usually feel awful, as they often feature adjusting devices let into the front torsion bars, which alter the steering geometry.

Brakes (including handbrake)

The disc brakes as fitted to Bays and T3s have the best feel, and usually stop the vehicle in a straight line, unless a calliper is seized. If drum brakes are adjusted correctly, they work satisfactorily but often have a tendency to pull to one side following the camber of the road. If you can feel a slight pulsing through the pedal, the Bus has distorted drums or discs. The handbrake, if adjusted correctly to about four or five clicks, is a very capable device, able to hold the Bus on quite steep hills.

Noises

Although hard to define, here are a few personal experiences. A broken crankshaft, most common with 30bhp engines, can be quiet at a certain speed, but make an awful row when travelling faster or slower. A broken piston makes a 'chang chang' sound, while a failed valve spring sounds like 'tak tak'. A scraping sound from the front, when cornering at town speeds, is often due to badly adjusted front wheel bearings, causing the front brakes to rub. A low rumble from the back end can be due to a worn rear wheel bearing. Buses with the double-jointed driveshafts 'click' when cornering if a constant velocity joint is about to fail. Most older Buses suffer from a bit of transmission whine, and this is particularly true of vehicles fitted with a crash box.

Performance
See 'Data' chart.

Oil pressure
If the oil pressure warning light comes on when driving, stop immediately and check the oil level, as the light only comes on when there is hardly any oil pressure left. A healthy air-cooled engine operates at 28psi maximum, although there is no way of checking this with the standard setup. Gauges are available from VDO, but they can make you paranoid!

Charging rate
As long as the generator warning light stays off when driving, you can assume that it's charging OK. If the warning light comes on when driving, stop immediately! You may have a broken fan belt, (which has serious consequences for the health of an air-cooled engine). The charging rate can be checked using a multimeter, along with the techniques outlined in a good workshop manual.

Controls
Apart from the pedals of Splitties and Bays standing upright with the pivot at floor level, all the major controls are similar to most vehicles of the era. A rotating knob facing forward under the front seat controls the heater of a Splittie, while Bay window models have three vertical levers situated on the dashboard to control heater and ventilation output. Additionally, Bays have a heater outlet set in the floor between the front seats to provide heat to the rear. Splitties built before June 1960 were fitted with a choke control knob adjacent to the heater control, this was abandoned when later carburettors featured an auto choke.

Switches
The Splittie is renowned for its simple yet functional dashboard. Very early barn door models were fitted with a simple instrument binnacle that doubled up as a steering column support. This housed a single speedometer dial in a plastic surround fitted with two-turn switches to control the lights and wipers. An additional switch in the centre of the dashboard controlled the semaphore indicators. March 1955 saw the introduction of a full-width dashboard, fitted with a removable panel to accommodate a radio, and pull switches to control lights and wipers. A stalk on the steering column controls the indicators. In August 1965, the lights and wipers were changed back to rotary switches.

The Bay dash has provision for three instrument dials. The central position houses the speedometer, while the petrol gauge and warning lights occupy the left dial. The right-hand dial is used for a clock in some models. The ignition/starter switch, combined with a steering lock, is located on the right-hand side of the steering column. Two steering column stalks are provided with the left one being for the indicators and headlamp dip function, and the right one controlling the windscreen wipers and screen wash. Soft feel switches along the lower edge of the dashboard control the lights and emergency flashers.

The T3 dashboard is similar to that of Golfs, Passats and Polos of the era. Rocker switches predominate, although slide controls operate the heater and ventilation system. Two stalks were multi-functional, but not quite as flimsy as their looks suggested. As with all plastic items, look out for damage caused by a combination of age and carelessness.

Ramp check

You may be able to persuade your local MoT or tyre depot to allow you to raise the Bus on a ramp for a better inspection of the underside. Refer to previous evaluation chapters for the appropriate information and then pay particular attention to the following.

Have an assistant sit in the Bus to press pedals and rock the steering. Inspect the flexible brake pipes for cracking on the outer casing, and check for bulging while your assistant presses the brake pedal. Check all the metal brake pipes for corrosion and signs of leaking. Have your assistant rock the steering while set straight-ahead, then in the right and left full lock positions. Check the track rod ball joints, steering box and swivel ball joints for excessive play.

Check the under-body and chassis for corrosion, paying particular attention to the girder sections at the front and rear. The floorpans, which protect the outriggers between the sills and chassis rails, are also prone to corrosion, if present. Check the battery tray as the presence of battery acid and the fumes created when the battery is being charged during normal use is a recipe for corrosion.

Look at the vertical panel behind the front wheel; if this has been welded it will probably look flat as, originally, the ends of the inner sill protrude by about four millimetres. On Splitties and Bays, check the condition of the flexible petrol pipe just forward of the left-hand heat exchanger. Failure of these flexible pipes, or the lack of hose clips, often results in barbecued Buses. Look for signs of a leaky petrol tank on a Bay, as they have been known to collapse due to breather and vacuum pipes being incorrectly connected, causing it to leak. Check for engine and transmission oil leaks. Pay attention to the rubber axle boots on the swing-axle equipped Splittie and the driveshaft gaiters on the double-jointed axle models. Inspect the exhaust at this point but be prepared to overlook its condition, due to limited lifespan and ease of replacement. If you are looking at an air-cooled model, heat exchangers aren't considered as part of the exhaust, are handed, sold singly, and relatively expensive.

Evaluation procedure

Add up the total points score: 196 = excellent, possibly Concours; 147 = good; 98 = average; 49 = poor. Cars scoring over 123 will be completely useable and will require only maintenance and care to keep in condition. Cars scoring between 49 and 97 will require full restoration (at much the same cost), cars scoring between 99 and 123 will require very careful assesment of necessary repair/restoration costs in order to reach a realistic value.

Auctions
– sold! Another way to buy your dream

Auction pros & cons

Pros: Prices will usually be lower than those of dealers or private sellers and you might grab a bargain. Auctioneers have usually established clear title with the seller. At the venue you can usually examine documentation relating to the vehicle.

Cons: You have to rely on a sketchy catalogue description of condition and history. The opportunity to inspect is limited, and you cannot drive the Bus. Such vehicles are often a little below par and may require some work. It's easy to overbid. There will usually be a buyer's premium in addition to the auction hammer price.

Which auction?

Auctions by established auctioneers are advertised in car magazines and on the auction houses' websites. A catalogue or a simple printed list of the lots for auction might only be available a day or two ahead, though often lots are listed and pictured on auctioneers' websites much earlier. Contact the auction company to ask if previous auction selling prices are available, as this is useful information (details of past sales are often available on websites).

Catalogue, entry fee and payment details

When you purchase the catalogue of the vehicles in the auction, it often acts as a ticket allowing two people to attend the viewing days and the auction. Catalogue details tend to be comparatively brief, but will include information such as 'one owner from new, low mileage, full service history', etc. It will also usually show a guide price to give you some idea of what to expect to pay and will tell you what is charged as a 'Buyer's premium'. The catalogue will also contain details of acceptable forms of payment. At the fall of the hammer an immediate deposit is usually required, the balance payable within 24 hours. If the plan is to pay by cash there may be a cash limit. Some auctions will accept payment by debit card. Sometimes credit or charge cards are acceptable, but will often incur an extra charge. A bank draft or bank transfer will have to be arranged in advance with your own bank as well as with the auction house. No vehicle will be released before all payments are cleared. If delays occur in payment then storage costs can accrue.

Buyer's premium

A buyer's premium will be added to the hammer price: don't forget this in your calculations. It is not usual for there to be a further state tax or local tax on the purchase price and/or on the buyer's premium.

Viewing

In some instances it's possible to view on the day, or days before, as well as in the hours prior to the auction. There are auction officials available who are willing to help out by opening engine and luggage compartments and to allow you to inspect the interior. While the officials may start the engine for you, a test drive is out of the question. Crawling under and around the Bus as much as you want is permitted, but you can't suggest that the Bus you are interested in be jacked up, or attempt to do the job yourself. You can also ask to see any documentation available.

Bidding
Before you take part in the auction, decide your maximum bid – and stick to it!

It may take a while for the auctioneer to reach the lot you are interested in, so use that time to observe how other bidders behave. When it's the turn of your vehicle, attract the auctioneer's attention and make an early bid. The auctioneer will then look to you for a reaction every time another bid is made, usually the bids will be in fixed increments until the bidding slows, when smaller increments will often be accepted before the hammer falls. If you want to withdraw from the bidding, make sure the auctioneer understands your intentions – a vigorous shake of the head when he or she looks to you for the next bid should do the trick.

Assuming that you are the successful bidder, the auctioneer will note your card or paddle number, and from that moment on you will be responsible for the vehicle.

If the Bus is unsold, either because it failed to reach the reserve or because there was little interest, it may be possible to negotiate with the owner, via the auctioneers, after the sale is over.

Successful bid
There are two more items to think about. How to get the Bus home, and insurance. If you can't drive the Bus, your own or a hired trailer is one way, another is to have the vehicle shipped using the facilities of a local company. The auction house will also have details of companies specialising in the transfer of all types of vehicle, including Buses.

Insurance for immediate cover can usually be purchased on site, but it may be more cost-effective to make arrangements in advance (don't forget classic vehicle insurance).

eBay & other online auctions?
eBay and other online auctions could land you a Bus at a bargain price, though you'd be foolhardy to bid without examining the vehicle first, something most vendors encourage. A useful feature of eBay is that the geographical location of the vehicle is shown, so you can narrow your choices to those within a realistic radius of home. Be prepared to be outbid in the last few moments of the auction. Remember, your bid is binding, and it will be very, very difficult to get restitution in the case of a crooked vendor fleecing you – caveat emptor!

Be aware that some vehicles offered for sale in online auctions are 'ghost' vehicles. Don't part with any cash without being sure that the Bus does actually exist and is as described (usually pre-bidding inspection is possible).

Auctioneers
See 'The community' chapter.

Paperwork
– correct documentation is essential!

The paper trail
The best Buses come with a large portfolio of paperwork accumulated and passed on by a succession of owners. This documentation represents the real history of the Bus, and from it can be deduced the care the Bus has received, how much it's been used, which specialists have worked on it, and details of repairs and restorations. All of this information is priceless, so be very wary of Buses with little paperwork.

Registration documents
All countries/states have some form of registration for private vehicles, whether it's like the American 'pink slip' system or the British 'log book' system.

Check that the registration document is genuine and relates to the Bus in question, and that all details are correct, including chassis/VIN and engine numbers. If buying from the previous owner, their name and address will be recorded in the document.

In the UK, the registration document (V5C) is printed in coloured sections. The blue part relates to the vehicle's specification, the green has details of the new owners and the black indicates what to do when selling the vehicle or changing other details. A small yellow section deals with selling the car within the motor trade.

The DVLA will provide details of earlier keepers of the vehicle upon payment of a small fee, and much can be learned in this way.

If the Bus has a foreign registration there may be expensive and time-consuming formalities to complete. Do you really want the hassle?

Roadworthiness certificate
Most country/state administrations require that vehicles are regularly tested to prove that they are safe to use on the public highway, and do not produce excessive emissions. In the UK, that test (the MoT) is carried out at approved testing stations, for a fee. In the USA, the requirement varies, but most states insist on an emissions test every two years as a minimum, while the police are charged with pulling over unsafe-looking vehicles.

In the UK, the test is required on an annual basis once a vehicle becomes three years old, but is no longer applicable if the vehicle was built before 1 Jan 1960. Of particular relevance for older cars is that the certificate issued includes the mileage reading recorded at the test date and, therefore, becomes an independent record of that vehicle's history. Ask the seller if previous certificates are available. Without an MoT the vehicle should be trailered to its new home, unless you insist that a valid MoT is part of the deal (not such a bad idea this, as you'll know the Bus was roadworthy on the day it was tested, and you won't need to wait for the old certificate to expire before having the test done).

Road licence
The administration of every country/state charges some kind of tax for the use of its

road system. The 'road licence,' and how it is displayed, varies enormously.

Whatever its form, the 'road licence' must relate to the vehicle carrying it, and must be present and valid if the vehicle is to be driven on the public highway. The value of the licence will depend on the length of time it's valid.

In the UK the requirement by law to display a tax disc has been discontinued. If a vehicle is untaxed because it has not been used for a period of time, the owner has to inform the licensing authorities, otherwise the vehicle's date-related registration number will be lost and there will be a lot of paperwork to get it re-registered. Also in the UK, vehicles manufactured before 1 Jan 1974 are currently tax exempt, however you still have to apply annually for vehicle tax. Clubs can often provide formal proof that a particular vehicle qualifies for this valuable concession.

Certificates of authenticity
For many makes of collectible vehicle it is possible to get a certificate proving the age and authenticity (eg engine and chassis numbers, paint colour and trim) – sometimes called 'Heritage Certificates.' If the vehicle has one of these, it's a definite bonus. If you want to obtain one, the relevant owners' club is the best starting point.

Valuation certificate
Hopefully, the vendor will have a recent valuation certificate or letter signed by a recognised expert stating how much he, or she, believes the particular Bus to be worth (such documents, together with photos, are usually needed to get 'agreed value' insurance). Such documents should act only as confirmation of your own assessment of the Bus rather than a guarantee of value, as the expert might not have seen the Bus. To obtain a formal valuation contact the owners' club.

Service history
Although most Buses will have been serviced at home for a good number of years, try to obtain as much service history and other paperwork pertaining to the Bus as you can. Dealer stamps or specialist garage receipts score most points in the value stakes. However, items like the original bill of sale, handbook, parts invoices and repair bills, add to the story and the character of the Bus. Even a brochure correct to the year of manufacture and original market is a useful document. If the seller claims that the Bus has been restored, expect receipts, etc, from a specialist restorer.

If the seller claims to have carried out regular servicing, ask what work was completed, when, and seek some evidence of it being carried out. Your assessment of the Bus' overall condition should tell you whether the seller's claims are genuine.

Restoration photographs
If the seller tells you that the Bus has been restored, then expect to be shown a series of photographs taken while the restoration was underway. Pictures taken at various stages, and from various angles, should help you gauge the thoroughness of the work. If you buy the Bus, ask if you can have all the photos (or quality copies) as they form an important part of the vehicle's history. It's surprising how many sellers are happy to part with their Bus and accept your cash, but want to hang on to their photos!

What's it worth to you?
– be realistic, head over heart!

Condition

The value of Splitties and Bays has been spiralling ever-upwards for many years, while the T3 has remained more or less static during the same period. The best sources for current prices are the small adverts in the VW magazines and their attendant websites. Similarly, sites such as www.thesamba.com are an ideal starting point (note that the Vanagon commands a higher price in the USA than does the T3 in Europe). Bear in mind that a Bus that is truly a recent show winner could be worth more than our highest suggestions. Assuming that the Bus you have in mind is not in show/Concours condition, then relate the level of condition that you judge the Bus to be in with the appropriate guide price. How does the figure compare with the asking price? Before you start haggling with the seller, consider what affect any variation from standard specification might have on the Bus's value.

If you're buying from a dealer, remember there will be a premium on the price.

Although we have already given what we believe to be realistic prices for all three generations of Bus, there are two additional factors to consider.

Is the value of Panelvans and Pickups, plus the numerous and sometimes obscure variants, such as hearses, mobile shops, or ladder trucks, the same as Kombis and Microbuses? Interesting though these vehicles are, what practical use can they be put to? Yes, they are Concours material, but is there much fun driving them at other times? On this basis, we would be tempted to value them slightly lower than Kombis and Microbuses.

Concours events invariably attract Campers, and owners go to extraordinary lengths to ensure that the interior is exactly as Westfalia, Devon, or whichever, intended. Particularly in Splittie guise, such a vehicle is worth a mint! However, many people want to buy a Camper to use as it was originally intended. This is where the need for originality has to be called into question. However, while a simple conversion by a leading manufacturer that sleeps two and hasn't a pop-top, or more so a homespun conversion, is likely to command less than a full blown four berth Camper, with pop top and awning, it is our view that all Campers should rightly command a higher price than the equivalent straightforward Microbus or Kombi.

Striking a deal

Negotiate on the basis of your condition assessment and fault rectification cost, whether it's a Splittie, Bay or T3, Possibly be wary of a T3 that needs restoration - your money might be better spent elsewhere. Also take into account the Bus' specification. Be realistic about the value, but don't be completely intractable; a small compromise on the part of the vendor or buyer will often facilitate a deal at little real cost.

Do you really want to restore?

– it'll take longer and cost more than you think ...

The biggest cost involved in any restoration project put into the hands of professionals, is not the parts you'll need, or the materials involved, but labour. Such restorations don't come cheap, while there are three other issues to consider when dealing with the trade.

First, make it abundantly clear what you want doing. It's no use simply indicating that the Bus needs to be restored. For example, are all replacement panels to be new old-stock, or at least correct for the year? Is a re-spray to be a bare metal one? Should all window glass be removed prior to painting? The list is endless if you are going to be fair to the professionals and, in turn, if they are to give you the result required.

In need of complete restoration, involving expensive front panel, replacement, doors, new window rubbers all round, and a first class paint job! Probably worth doing because of age and general desirability.

Secondly, make sure that not only is a detailed estimate involved, but also that it is more or less binding. There are too many stories of a person quoted one figure only to be presented with an invoice for a far larger one!

Thirdly, check that the company you are dealing with has a good reputation. There have been quite well known names in years gone by whose work has later been shown to be disappointing, at best. You don't want to be faced with the prospect of having a Bus restored for a second time.

Restoring a Bus yourself requires a number of skills, which if you already have them is marvellous, but acquiring the same might not be an overnight process. Can you weld; can you prepare and spray a vehicle as big as a Bus yourself; can you rebuild an engine; and have you got the equipment? Of course, you might elect to oversee a project but have you sufficient friends with the expertise to accomplish all you require? Above all, have your contacts got time to do the jobs you want according to the schedule you set.

Be prepared for a top-notch professional to put you on a lengthy waiting list or, if tackling a restoration yourself, expect things to go wrong and set aside extra time to complete the task. We can think of people who have taken over two years to restore what wasn't an absolute basket case, and of at least one other who pushed things through in well under a year ... at the cost of his marriage.

Some go for a rolling restoration (not a good idea if Concours is the goal), while all year usage with panels in primer will cause deterioration, especially if there is salt about. The biggest danger of all with either rolling restorations or hobby-based projects, is one of loss of interest, as either the project drags out, or the icy garage becomes more inhospitable! How many Buses do you see advertised as 'unfinished projects'? Part-finished Buses inevitably spell financial loss, while many can be quite difficult to move on.

A rusty and battered T3 isn't worth restoring currently as values don't warrant the necessary outlay. Beware the T3 that has been given a quick makeover.

This immaculate Samba has been fully restored at considerable expense. The work included fitting a 'new' roof panel, but the time and expense involved was worth it, as the vehicle is now valued at a substantial figure.

Heavy frontal impact could easily have caused costly damage to areas like the cab step. The bumper, front panel, etc, would need replacing. In the 1990s it wouldn't have been worth it, but it certainly is now.

Paint faults

– a bad complexion, including dimples, pimples and bubbles ...

Paint faults generally occur due lack of protection/maintenance, or to poor preparation prior to a respray or touch-up. Some of the following conditions may be present in the vehicle you're looking at:

Orange peel

This appears as an uneven paint surface, similar to the appearance of the skin of an orange. The fault is caused by the failure of atomised paint droplets to flow into each other when they hit the surface. It's sometimes possible to rub out the effect with proprietary paint cutting/rubbing compound or very fine grades of abrasive paper. A respray may be necessary in severe cases. Consult a bodywork repairer/paint shop for advice on the particular vehicle.

Cracking

Severe cases are likely to have been caused by too heavy an application of paint (or filler beneath the paint). Also, insufficient stirring of the paint before application can lead to the components being improperly mixed, and cracking can result. Incompatibility with the paint already on the panel can have a similar effect. To rectify it is necessary to rub down to a smooth, sound finish before respraying the problem area.

Cracking due to filler under paint lifting.

Crazing

Sometimes the paint takes on a crazed rather than a cracked appearance when the problems mentioned under 'Cracking' are present. This problem can also be caused by a reaction between the underlying surface and the paint. Paint removal and respraying the problem area is usually the only solution.

Blistering

Almost always caused by corrosion of the metal beneath the paint. Usually perforation will be found in the metal and the damage will usually be worse than that suggested by the area of blistering. The metal will have to be repaired before repainting.

Micro blistering

Usually the result of an economy respray where inadequate heating has allowed moisture to settle on the vehicle before spraying. Consult a paint specialist, but damaged paint will have to be removed before partial or full respraying. Can also be caused by vehicle covers that don't 'breathe'.

Blistering caused by rust coming through from an internal panel joint.

Fading

Some colours, especially reds, are prone to fading if subject to strong sunlight for long periods without the benefit of polish protection. Sometimes proprietary paint restorers and/or paint cutting/rubbing compounds will retrieve the situation. Often a respray is the only real solution.

'Pimples' of rust originating from dampness in the respray process, or rust on a panel before paint application.

Peeling

Often a problem with metallic paintwork when the sealing lacquer becomes damaged and begins to peel off. Poorly applied paint may also peel. The remedy is to strip and start again!

Dimples

Dimples in the paintwork are caused by the residue of polish (particularly silicone types) not being removed properly before respraying. Paint removal and repainting is the only solution.

The lacquer is peeling causing problems with paint beneath.

Dents

Small dents are usually easily cured by the 'Dentmaster', or equivalent process, that sucks or pushes out the dent (as long as the paint surface is still intact). Companies offering dent removal services usually come to your home – consult your telephone directory.

Lack of use problems
– just like their owners, Buses need exercise!

Buses, like humans, are at their most efficient if they exercise regularly. A run of at least 10 miles, once a week, is recommended for classics.

Seized components
Pistons in callipers, slave and master cylinders can seize. The clutch may seize if the plate becomes stuck to the flywheel because of corrosion. Handbrakes (parking brakes) can seize if the cables and linkages rust. Pistons can seize in the bores due to corrosion.

Fluids
Old, acidic oil can corrode bearings. Check the oil on the dipstick. If the engine has not run for some time, it's likely that the carbon and sludge that was suspended in the oil has now settled out as a black acidic deposit on all the internal surfaces. This can usually be sorted with an oil change, followed by another after 500 gently driven miles. In a worst-case scenario, the acid in the oil could have attacked the crankshaft and other engine bearings, resulting in trouble further down the line.

Uninhibited coolant can corrode internal waterways. Lack of antifreeze can cause core plugs to be pushed out, even cracks in the block or head. Silt settling and solidifying can cause overheating.

Brake fluid absorbs water from the atmosphere and should be renewed every two years. Old fluid with a high water content can cause corrosion and pistons/callipers to seize (freeze) and can cause brake failure when the water turns to vapour near hot braking components.

Tyre problems
Tyres that have had the weight of the Bus on them in a single position for some time will develop flat spots, resulting in some (usually temporary) vibration. The tyre walls may have cracks or (blister-type) bulges, meaning new tyres are needed.

Shock absorbers (dampers)
Until March 1955, lever arm shock absorbers were fitted to the rear; all other applications are fitted with the telescopic type. Buses that have been idle for some time often suffer from seal breakdown, resulting in fluid loss. Check each shock absorber for fluid loss and then press down on each corner to check efficiency. Once released, the Bus should return to normal ride height without bouncing further. Malfunction of either test would result in an MoT failure. Apart from the above points, Volkswagen shock absorbers give a long service life.

Tyres that have been flat for some time will need replacing, due to irreparable damage to the sidewalls.

Rubber and plastic

Window and door seals can harden and leak. Gaiters/boots can crack. Wiper blades will harden.

Electrics

The battery will be of little use if it has not been charged for many months.

A rotten exhaust isn't a problem as it's cheap to replace. This Beetle exhaust is similar to a Splittie's or Bay's.

Earthing/grounding problems are common when the connections have corroded. Ceramic continental fuses may rust/corrode and will need to be cleaned with fine grain emery paper and sprayed with electrical cleaning fluid. Most circuits use 6.3mm spade connectors, which can be cleaned in the same way to maintain peak efficiency and avoid voltage drops, particularly on 6-volt Splitties (pre-1967 model year).

Sparkplug electrodes will often have corroded in an unused engine.

Wiring insulation can harden and fail.

Rotting exhaust system

Exhaust gas contains a high water content so exhaust systems corrode very quickly from the inside when the Bus is not used. Expect to replace the exhaust system on a Bus that has stood idle for 6 months or more.

Perished window seals often conceal frame rust due to water ingress.

Auctioneers

Barrett-Jackson – www.barrett-jackson.com
Bonhams – www.bonhams.com
British Car Auctions (BCA) – www.bca-europe.com/www.british-car-auctions.co.uk
Cheffins – www.cheffins.co.uk
Christies – www.christies.com
Coys – www.coys.co.uk
eBay – www.ebay.com
H&H – www.classic-auctions.co.uk
RM – www.rmauctions.com
Shannons – www.shannons.com.au
Silver – www.silverauctions.com

Clubs across the world

Canada
Club international de camping-car Westfalia
PO Box 47101, Sillery (Quebec), G1S 4X1. www.westfalia.qc.ca

Germany
VW-Bus-Club Koblenz
Manfred Klee, Erlenweg 11, D – 56323 Waldesch
Tel: +49 (0) 2628/2428. Fax: +49 (0) 2628/987787. E-mail: mm.klee@vwbc.de. www.vwbc.de

Bulli Kartei
BulliKartei is the worldwide club for all friends of the Splittie 1950–1967. Membership is not restricted to ownership: to be interested and to like these vehicles is enough to become a BulliKartei member!
H. Joachim Brauer, President, Seveckenhof 2, D-58455 Witten (Heven), Germany.

www.bullikartei.de E-mail: mail@bullikartei.de

Japan
VW owners club KdF of Japan
Atsushi Nobusawa. '66 Westy owner in Japan, E-mail: 3s@kakaa.or.jp

Switzerland
Westfalia-Interessengemeinschaft Schweiz
Established in 1988 we currently have 36 members (1999). Most members drive a Joker Typ1 or 2, some on the VW-LT-base. The oldest one dates from 1976. E-mail: hr@trosoft.ch

UK
Cornwall Volkswagen Owners Club
Cornwall, UK.
www.cvwoc.co.uk

Volkswagen Owners Club (Great Britain)
The oldest VW club in Britain. While some members join to find out more about later water-cooled models, both Buses and Beetles play an important part in the club's make-up.
PO Box 7, Burntwood, Staffs. WS7 2SB. Tel 01952 242167.
www.vwocgb.com

Club 80-90
Web-based club for owners of T3s
E-mail: andy@club80-90.co.uk.
www.club80-90.co.uk

VW Camping Club (GB)
Peter Philips, 101 Lodge Road, Long Eaton, Nottingham, NG10 1AP.

Tel: 01159 726980.

Type 2 Owners Club
57 Humphrey Avenue, Charford,
Bromsgrove, Worcestershire, B60 3JD.
Tel: +44 (0)1527 872194.
Fax: +44 (0)1527 872194.
www.vwt2oc.co

SSVC – Split Screen Van Club
For owners or would-be owners.
www.ssvc.org.uk
E-mail: membership@ssvc.org.uk

USA
A Hawaiian Bus Club
Shayne Sakoda. Email: HawaiianRoller@
msn.com

Late Model Bus Organization, International (LiMBO)
An organization dedicated to post-
1967 VW Type IIs including Vanagons
& Eurovans! Membership in LiMBO
(which includes a subscription to The
Transporter) is $20 per year. Contact
the address below for subscription rates
outside the United States.
LiMBO, c/o Dale Ward, 9 Golden Hill
Ave, Shewsbury MA. 01545. Tel: (413)
743-1814. www.limbobus.org

Specialists
There are so many Bus businesses
that we have restricted our listing to
UK names. This list does not imply
recommendation and is not deemed to
be comprehensive.

Alan H Schofield (parts)
Unit 14, Dinting Lane, Glossop,
Derbyshire, SK13 7NU. Tel: 01457
854267.
www.ahschofield.co.uk

Custom Classic Retro
Bespoke VW interior specialists.
Tel 01509 558616
www.customclassicretro.co.uk

VW Heritage Parts Centre (parts)
 47 Dolphin Road, Shoreham-By-Sea,
West Sussex, BN43 6PB.
Tel 01273 444 045
www.vwheritage.com

Karmann Konnection (parts and some Bus sales)
289 Victoria Avenue, Southend on Sea,
SS2 6NE. Tel 01702 340 613
www.karmannkonnection.com

German Swedish & French (parts)
Branches all over the country. Tel: 020
8917 3866. www.gsfcarparts.com

Burt's Bus Emporium
3-5 South Street, Woolacombe, EX34
7BB. Tel 01271 871 510
http://www.burtsbusemporium.co.uk/
info@burtsbusemporium.co.uk

KombiKlassics (restoration, spares)
Unit 2, John's Road, Carey, Wareham,
Dorset BH20 4BG. Tel: 01929 553336.
www.kombiklassics.co.uk

VW BulliBarn
Campers bought and sold.
Unit 3, Gosbecks Farm, Gosbecks
Road, Colchester, Essex CO2 9JT.
Tel: 01206 563433.
http://www.vwbullibarn.co.uk/
vwbullibarn@btconnect.com

Just Kampers
Parts, accessories and insurance.
Tel: 0845 1204712.
www.justkampers.com

Calypso Campers
Custom built interiors.
18 Paul's Dene Crescent, Salisbury,
Wiltshire, SP1 3QU.
Tel: 01722 327081.
Mob: 07720 167603.
www.calypsocampers.co.uk

mpicampers
Camper sales 1968 to 1990.
Lon Parc wr, Ruthin, LL15 1NJ.
Tel: 01824 705 600
 www.mpicampers.co.uk

Paris Beetles
Sunroofs for Buses
Little Orchard, King Street, High Ongar,
Essex, CM5 9NS. Tel: 01277 823365.
www.vwbullibarn.co.uk

Volksheaven
VW salvage.
Hop Hills Lane, Dunscroft, Doncaster,
DN7 4JX.
Tel: 01302 351355.
www.volksheaven.co.uk

Cornwall Campers
Camper hire.
Carnebo Farm, Goohhavern, Truro,
Cornwall, TR4 9QH

Tel 01872 571988.
www.cornwallcampers.co.uk

Cogbox
Gearbox rebuilds and repairs.
Tel: 0208 842 2580 (London area)

Richard Hulin
Repairs and spares.
Tel: 01452 502333 (Gloucester)

Stateside Tuning
Engine machining and tuning specialist.

Tel: 01608 812438 (Moreton-in-Marsh,
Gloucester)

Wolfsburg West
www.wolfsburgwest.com

Books
The Volkswagen Bus Book– Malcolm
Bobbitt, Veloce, 2007.

*VW Bus – 40 years of Splitties,
Bays and T3s* – Richard Copping,
Veloce, 2006. History and marketing –
including Campers – unique brochure
style.

*VW Transporter and Microbus
Specification Guide 1950–1967* – David
Eccles, Crowood Press, 2002.

*VW Transporter and Microbus
Specification Guide 1967–979*
– Alexander Prinz & Vince Molenarar,
Crowood, 2005. History, detailed
specification year-by-year, specials.

*VW Camper – The Inside Story 1952-
2005* – David Eccles, Crowood Press,
2005. 40 different camper conversions,
range of models and interiors.

Volkswagen Transporter – Jonathan
Harvey, Haynes, 2008

*Volkswagen Transporter The Legendary
Type 2, 1950–982* – Laurence Meredith,
Crowood, 2005.

*Splittie, Bay and air-cooled T3.
Original VW Bus* – Laurence Meredith,
Bay View Books, 1997. (Out of print)
Restoration guide to all Splitties and
Bays, excluding Campers.

Volkswagen Transporter 1950–1990

– Richard Copping & Ken Cservenka, Nostalgia Road, 2005. Potted history including Campers, range explained.
VW Transporter/Bus 1949-1967 – Walter Zeichner, Schiffer Publishing Ltd, 1989. Illustrated history.

VW-Campingwagen 1951-1991 – Michael Steinke, Schrader Verlag, 2003. German text – Campers.

Volkswagen Model History – Joachim Kuch, Haynes Publishing, 1999. All boxer engine VWs. Splittie, Bay and T3 (including water-cooled).

Volkswagen Bus Camper Van Performance Portfolio, 1954–1967, Brookland Books
Volkswagen Bus Camper Van Performance Portfolio, 1968–1979, Brookland Books
Volkswagen Bus Camper Van Performance Portfolio, 1979–1991, Brookland Books.
Three volumes of reprints of contemporary reviews from around the world.

Volkswagen Transporter – The First 60 Years – Richard Copping with Brian Screaton, Haynes, 2009

VW Camper and Microbus – Richard Copping, Shire Library, 2009

Owners Workshop Manuals, Haynes. A series of Bus workshops manuals published by Haynes. Invaluable to the home mechanic.
Robert Bentley Manuals, USA. Reprints of factory manuals.

Volkswagen T3 Transporter, Caravelle, Camper and Vanagon 1979-1992 – Richard Copping, Crowood 2011

Vital statistics
– essential data at your fingertips

Number built
Splittie: 1,833,000
Bay: 2,465,000
T3: 1,839,000

It's impossible to assess every engine variation over 40 years of production. Therefore, we've picked three models, a late 1500cc Splittie, a 1600cc early Bay, and a 2.0-litre air-cooled T3.

Performance
1966 Splittie: Max and cruising speed 65mph
1971 Bay: Max and cruising speed 68mph, 0-50 – 23.0 seconds
1980 T3: Max and cruising speed 80mph, 0-60 – 18.0 seconds

Engine
1966 Splittie: Air-cooled horizontally opposed flat four – 1493cc. Bore and stroke 83 x 69mm. Compression ratio 7.5:1. 42bhp @ 3800rpm
1971 Bay: Air-cooled horizontally opposed flat four – 1584cc. Bore and stroke 85.5 x 69mm. Compression ratio 7.7:1. 50bhp @ 4000rpm
1980 T3: Air-cooled horizontally opposed flat four – 1970cc. Bore and stroke 94 x 71mm. Compression ratio 7.4:1. 70bhp @ 4200rpm

Gearbox
1966 Splittie: Four speed manual. Ratios – first 3.80:1, second 2.06:1, third 1.22:1, fourth 0.82:1
1971 Bay: Synchronised 4-speed manual. Ratios – first 3.80:1, second 2.06:1, third 1.26:1, fourth 0.89:1
1980 T3: Synchronised 4-speed manual (or 3-speed automatic). Ratios – first 3.78:1, second 2.06:1, third 1.26:1, fourth 0.852:1

Brakes
1966 Splittie – Hydraulic. Drums all round
1971 Bay – Hydraulic – discs up front
1980 T3 – Hydraulic – discs up front

Electrics
1966 Splittie: 6-volt
1971 Bay: 12-volt
1980 T3: 12-volt

Dimensions
1966 Splittie: Length 403.5cm, width 167.5cm, height 186.88cm
1971 Bay: Length 443.5cm, width 169.25cm, height 193cm
1980 T3: Length 457.5cm, width 180.5cm, height 195.4cm

Wheelbase
1966 Splittie: 240cm
1971 Bay: 236.25cm
1980 T3: 246cm

Fuel consumption
1966 Splittie: 28mpg
1971 Bay: 24.8mpg
1980 T3: 21mpg

Major change points by date
1953 March: Synchromesh on 2nd, 3rd, and top gears.
1953 Dec: Introduction of 30bhp engine (previously 25bhp).
1955 March: Re-vamped design: peaked cab roof for better ventilation, much smaller engine lid, direct access

to interior from new tailgate (only Samba before).

1956 March: Production transferred in stages from Wolfsburg to new Hanover factory.

1959 May: Re-designed 30bhp engine, compression ratio increased.

1960 June: New engine – 34bhp.

1960 June: European models join US versions as semaphore bows out in favour of flashing indicators (US flashers from 1955).

1961 July 31: Fuel gauge fitted.

1962 Aug: Front bench seat replaced by separate seats for driver and passengers.

1963 Jan: New 1500 engine, initially only available for US market – from March elsewhere as an option.

1963 Aug: Wider rear window in re-designed tailgate.

1963 Aug: Flatter and rounder front indicators already fitted to US models from 1961, now universal.

1965 Autumn: 1200 engine finally phased out in all markets.

1966 Aug: 12-volt electrics.

1967 July 31st: End of Splittie production.

1967 Aug: Bay with single port 1600 engine.

1970 Aug: Front disc brakes, revised wheel design, but still 5-stud.

1970 Aug: Twin-port 1600 engine.

1971 Aug: 1700 engine introduced (Standard on all models US) Twin carburettors.

1972 Aug: Re-vamped front end with indicators above headlamps. Revised, sturdier bumpers. Front VW roundel reduced in size (3-speed automatic available with 1700 engine).

1973 Aug: 1800 engine replaces 1700. Bosch fuel injection for US models.

1975 July: Arrival of cloth upholstery

for Microbus ... but not all markets.

1975 Aug: 2 litre engine replaces 1800.

1979 July 31st: End of Bay production.

1979 Aug: T3 available with suitcase style 1600, 50bhp plus 2-litre, 70bhp air-cooled engines (US T3 marketed as Vanagon).

1980 Sept: 1.6 litre 50bhp diesel engine introduced (borrowed from the Golf).

1981 Sept: Arrival of first Caravelle luxury special edition.

1982 Sept: Two 1.9-litre water-cooled Boxer engines, 60 and 78bhp respectively replace air-cooled variants. 5-speed box also available.

1983 Sept: Marketing strategy – move over to Panelvans, Pickups and Kombis being known as Transporters, while Microbuses become Caravelle, available in C, CL and GL trim levels (Vanagon remains US name). (1.9-litre 90bhp fuel injected engine for special Carat model).

1985 Feb: Syncro permanent 4-wheel drive available on Transporters.

1985 Aug: 1.6 litre 70bhp turbo-diesel engine, plus 2.1-litre fuel-injected petrol engine producing 112bhp.

1986 Sept: Introduction of 'Multivan' – initially built by Westfalia – camper/bus.

1987 Sept: Non-turbo diesel ... bore increase. 1.7-litre, 57bhp, previously 50bhp.

1989 Sept: Double rectangular headlamps now on all models.

1990 Aug: Introduction of new T4 model – Syncro T3 continues until Sept 1992.

The Essential Buyer's Guide™ series ...

978-1-845840-22-8

978-1-845840-26-6

978-1-845840-29-7

978-1-845840-77-8

978-1-845840-99-0

978-1-904788-70-6

978-1-845841-01-0

978-1-845841-19-5

978-1-845841-13-3

978-1-845841-35-5

978-1-845841-36-2

978-1-845841-38-6

978-1-845841-46-1

978-1-845841-47-8

978-1-845841-63-8

978-1-845841-65-2

978-1-845841-88-1

978-1-845841-92-8

978-1-845842-00-0

978-1-845842-04-8

978-1-845842-05-5

978-1-845842-70-3

978-1-845842-81-9

978-1-845842-83-3

978-1-845842-84-0

978-1-845842-87-I

978-1-84584-134-8

978-1-845843-03-8

978-1-845843-09-0

978-1-845843-16-8

978-1-845843-29-8

978-1-845843-30-4

978-1-845843-34-2

978-1-845843-38-0

978-1-845843-39-7

978-1-845841-61-4

978-1-845842-31-4

978-1-845843-07-6

978-1-845843-40-3

978-1-845843-48-9

978-1-845843-63-2

978-1-845844-09-7

Index